C. W Whistler

King Alfred's Viking

C. W Whistler

King Alfred's Viking

ISBN/EAN: 9783743317239

Manufactured in Europe, USA, Canada, Australia, Japa

Cover: Foto ©ninafisch / pixelio.de

Manufactured and distributed by brebook publishing software (www.brebook.com)

C. W Whistler

King Alfred's Viking

The Project Gutenberg EBook of King Alfred's Viking, by Charles W. Whistl

This eBook is for the use of anyone anywhere at no cost and with
almost no restrictions whatsoever. You may copy it, give it away or
re-use it under the terms of the Project Gutenberg License included
with this eBook or online at www.gutenberg.net

Title: King Alfred's Viking
       A Story of the First English Fleet

Author: Charles W. Whistler

Release Date: November 13, 2004 [EBook #14034]
[Date last updated: July 28, 2006]

Language: English

Character set encoding: ASCII

*** START OF THIS PROJECT GUTENBERG EBOOK KING ALFRED'S VIKING ***

Produced by Martin Robb

KING ALFRED'S VIKING

A Story of the First English Fleet

by
Charles W. Whistler.

Contents

PREFACE.
CHAPTER I. THE SEEKING OF SWORD HELMBITER.
CHAPTER II. THE GIFTS OF TWO HEROES.
CHAPTER III. ODDA, THE EALDORMAN OF DEVON.
CHAPTER IV. JARL OSMUND'S DAUGHTER.

CHAPTER V. TWO MEETINGS IN ENGLAND.
CHAPTER VI. ALFRED THE KING.
CHAPTER VII. THE PIXIES' DANCE.
CHAPTER VIII. THE BLACK TWELFTH-NIGHT.
CHAPTER IX. THE SIGN OF ST. CUTHBERHT.
CHAPTER X. ATHELNEY AND COMBWICH.
CHAPTER XI. THE WINNING OF "THE RAVEN."
CHAPTER XII. EDINGTON FIGHT.
CHAPTER XIII. THE GREATEST VICTORY.
CHAPTER XIV. KING ALFRED'S WILL.
NOTES.

Preface.

The general details and course of events given in this story are, so far as regards the private life and doings of King Alfred, from his life as written by his chaplain, Asser. One or two further incidents of the Athelney period are from the later chroniclers--notably the sign given by St. Cuthberht--as are also the names of the herdsman and the nobles in hiding in the fen.

That Alfred put his first fleet into the charge of "certain Vikings" is well known, though the name of their chief is not given. These Vikings would certainly be Norse, either detached from the following of Rolf Ganger, who wintered in England in 875 A.D. the year before his descent on Normandy; or else independent rovers who, like Rolf, had been driven from Norway by the high-handed methods of Harald Fairhair. Indeed, the time when a Norse contingent was not present with the English forces, from this period till at least that of the battle of Brunanburh in 947 A.D. would probably be an exception.

There are, therefore, good historic grounds for the position given to the hero of the story as leader of the newly-formed fleet. The details of the burning of his supposed father's hall, and of the Orkney period, are from the Sagas.

Much controversy has raged over the sites of Ethandune and the landing place of Hubba at Kynwith Castle, owing probably to the duplication of names in the district where the last campaign took place. The story, therefore, follows the identifications given by the late Bishop Clifford in "The Transactions of the Somerset Archaeological Society" for 1875 and other years, as, both from topographic and strategic points of view, no other coherent identification seems possible.

The earthworks of the Danish position still remain on Edington hill, that looks out from the Polden range over all the country of Alfred's last refuge, and the bones of Hubba's men lie everywhere under the turf where they made their last stand under the old walls and earthworks of Combwich fort; and a lingering tradition yet records the extermination of a Danish force in the neighbourhood. Athelney needs but the cessation of today's drainage to revert in a very few years to what it was in Alfred's time--an island, alder covered, barely rising from fen and mere, and it needs but little imagination to reproduce what Alfred saw when, from the same point where one must needs be standing, he planned the final stroke that his people believed was inspired directly from above.

It would seem evident from Alfred's method with Guthrum that he realized that this king was but one among many leaders, and not directly responsible for the breaking of the solemn peace sworn at Exeter and Wareham. His position as King of East Anglia has gained him an ill reputation in the pages of the later chronicles; but neither Asser nor the *Anglo-Saxon Chronicle*-

-our best authorities--blames him as they, for his contemporaries knew him to be but a "host king," with no authority over newcomers or those who did not choose to own allegiance to him.

Save in a few cases, where the original spelling preserves a lost pronunciation, as in the first syllable of "Eadmund," the modern and familiar forms of the names have been used in preference to the constantly-varying forms given by the chroniclers. Bridgwater has no Saxon equivalent, the town being known only as "The Bridge" since the time when the Romans first fortified this one crossing place of the Parret; and the name of the castle before which Hubba fell varies from Cynuit through Kynwith to Kynwich, whose equivalent the Combwich of today is. Guthrum's name is given in many forms, from Gytro to Godramnus. Nor has it been thought worth while to retain the original spelling AElfred, the ae diphthong having been appropriated by us to an entirely new sound; while our own pronunciation of the name slightly broadened as yet in Wessex, is correct enough.

The exact relationship of St. Neot to Alfred, beyond that he was a close kinsman, is very doubtful. He has been identified with a brother, Athelstan of East Anglia, who is known to have retired to Glastonbury; but there is no more than conjecture, and I have been content with "cousinship."

C. W. Whistler

Stockland, 1898.

Chapter I. The Seeking of Sword Helmbiter.

Men call me "King Alfred's Viking," and I think that I may be proud of that name; for surely to be trusted by such a king is honour enough for any man, whether freeman or thrall, noble or churl. Maybe I had rather be called by that name than by that which was mine when I came to England, though it was a good title enough that men gave me, if it meant less than it seemed. For being the son of Vemund, king of Southmereland in Norway, I was hailed as king when first I took command of a ship of my own. Sea king, therefore, was I, Ranald Vemundsson, but my kingdom was but over ship and men, the circle of wide sea round me was nought that I could rule over, if I might seem to conquer the waves by the kingship of good seaman's craft.

One may ask how I came to lose my father's kingdom, which should have been mine, and at last to be content with a simple English earldom; or how it was that a viking could be useful to Alfred, the wise king. So I will tell the first at once, and the rest may be learned from what comes after.

If one speaks to me of Norway, straightway into my mind comes the remembrance of the glare of a burning hall, of the shouts of savage warriors, and of the cries of the womenfolk, among whom I, a ten-year-old boy, was when Harald Fairhair sent the great Jarl Rognvald and his men to make an end of Vemund, my father. For Harald had sworn a great oath to subdue all the lesser kings in the land and rule there alone, like Gorm in Denmark and Eirik in Sweden. So my father's turn came, and as he feasted with his ninety stout courtmen, the jarl landed under cover of the dark and fell on him, surrounding the house and firing it. Then was fierce fighting as my father and his men sallied again and again from the doors and were driven back, until the high roof fell in and there was a sudden silence, and an end.

Then in the silence came my mother's voice from where she stood on the balcony of the living house across the garth [iii]. I mind that she neither wept nor shrieked as did the women round her, and her voice was clear and strong over the roaring of the flames. I mind, too, the flash of helms and armour as every man turned to look on her who spoke.

"Coward and nidring art thou, Rognvald, who dared not meet Vemund, my husband, in open field, but must slay him thus. Ill may all things go with thee, till thou knowest what a burning hall is like for thyself. I rede thee to the open hillside ever, rather than come beneath a roof; for as thou hast wrought this night, so shall others do to thee."

Then rose a growl of wrath from Rognvald's men, but the great Jarl bade them cease, and harm none in all the place. So he went down to his ships with no more words and men said that he was ill at ease and little content, for he had lost as many men as he had slain, so stoutly fought my father and our courtmen, and had earned a curse, moreover, which would make his nights uneasy for long enough.

Then as he went my mother bade me look well at him, that in days to come I might know on whom to avenge my father's death. After that she went to her own lands in the south, for she was a jarl's daughter, and very rich.

Not long thereafter Harald Fairhair won all the land, and then began the trouble of ruling it; and men began to leave Norway because of the new laws, which seemed hard on them, though they were good enough.

Now two of Jarl Rognvald's sons had been good friends of my father before these troubles began, and one, Sigurd, had been lord over the Orkney Islands, and had died there. The other, Jarl Einar, fell out with Rognvald, his father, and we heard that he would take to the viking path, and go to the Orkneys, to win back the jarldom that Sigurd's death had left as a prey to masterless men and pirates of all sorts. So my mother took me to him, and asked him for the sake of old friendship to give me a place in his ship; for I was fourteen now, and well able to handle weapons, being strong and tall for my age, as were many of the sons of the old kingly stocks.

So Einar took me, having had no part in his father's doings towards us, and hating them moreover. He promised to do all that he might towards making a good warrior and seaman of me; and he was ever thereafter as a foster father to me, for my own had died in the hall with Vemund. It was his wish to make amends thus, if he could, for the loss his folk had caused me.

Of the next five years I need speak little, for in them I learned the viking's craft well. We won the Orkneys from those who held them, and my first fight was in Einar's ship, against two of the viking's vessels. After that we dwelt in Sigurd's great house in Kirkwall, and made many raids on the Sutherland and Caithness shores. I saw some hard fighting there, for the Scots are no babes at weapon play.

Then when I was nineteen, and a good leader, as they said, the words that my mother spoke to Jarl Rognvald came true, and he died even as he had slain my father.

For Halfdan and Gudrod, Harald Fairhair's sons, deeming that the Jarl stood in their way to power in Norway, burned him in his hall by night, and so my feud was at an end. But the king would in nowise forgive his sons for the slaying of his friend, and outlawed them. Whereon Halfdan came and fell on us in the Orkneys; and that was unlucky for him, for we beat him, and Jarl Einar avenged on him his father's death.

Now through this it came to pass that I saw Norway for the last time, for I went thither in Einar's best ship to learn if Harald meant to make the Orkneys pay for the death of his son-- which was likely, for a son is a son even though he be an outlaw.

So I came to my mother's place first of all, and full of joy and pleasant thoughts was I as we sailed into the well-remembered fiord to seek the little town at its head. And when we came there, nought but bitterest sorrow and wrath was ours; for the town was a black heap of ruin, and the few men who were left showed me where the kindly hands of the hill folk had laid my mother, the queen, in a little mound, after the Danish vikings, who had fallen suddenly on the place with fire and sword, had gone. They had grown thus bold because the great jarl was dead, and the king's sons had left the land without defence.

There I swore vengeance for this on every viking of Danish race that I might fall in with; for I was wild with grief and rage, as one might suppose. I set up a stone over the grave of my mother, graving runes thereon that should tell who she was and also who raised it; for I was skilled in the runic lore, having learned much from one of Einar's older men who had known my father.

Thereafter we cruised among the islands northwards until we learned that Harald was indeed upon us, and then I saw my last of Norway as we headed south again, and the last hilltop sank beneath the sea's rim astern of us. I did not know that so it would be at that time--it is well that one sees not far into things to come--but even now all my home seemed to be with Einar; and that also was not to last long, as things went. How that came about I must tell, for the end was that I came to Alfred the king.

When we came back to Kirkwall, I told the jarl all that I had done and learned; and grieved for me he was when he heard of my mother's death. Many things he said to me at that time which made him dearer to me. Then after a while he spoke of Harald, who, as it seemed, might come at any time.

"We cannot fight Norway," he said, "so we must even flit hence to the mainland and wait until Harald is tired of seeking us. It is in my mind that he seeks not so much for revenge as for payment of scatt from our islands. Now he has a reason for taking it by force. He will seek to fine us, and then make plans by which I shall hold the jarldom from him for yearly dues."

So he straightway called the Thing [iii] of all the Orkney folk, who loved him well, and put the matter before them; and they set to work and did his bidding, driving the cattle inland and scattering them, and making the town look as poor as they might.

Then in three days' time we sailed away laughing; for none but poor-looking traders were left, and no man would think that never had the Orkneys been so rich as in Einar's time. And he bade them make peace with the king when he came, and told them that so all would be well, for Harald would lay no heavy weregild on so poor a place for his son's slaying.

Southward we went to Caithness, and so westward along the Sutherland coast; for we had taken no scatt there for this year, and Einar would use this cruise to do so, seeing that we must put to sea. We were not the first who had laid these shores under rule from the Orkneys, for Jarl Sigurd had conquered them, meeting his death at last in a Sutherland firth, after victory, in a strange way.

He fought with a Scottish chief named Melbrigda of the Tusks, and slew him, and bore back his head to the ships at his saddle bow. Then the great teeth of the chief swung against the jarl's leg and wounded it, and of that he died, and so was laid in a great mound at the head of the firth where his ships lay. After that, the Orkneys were a nest of evil vikings till we came.

So it had happened that, from the time when it was made over him, Jarl Sigurd's mound had been untended, for we ourselves had never been so far south as this firth before. Indeed, it had been so laid waste by Sigurd's men after his death that there was nought to go there for. But at this time we had reason for getting into some quiet, unsought place where we should not be likely to be heard of, for the king had over-many ships and men for us to meet. So after a week's cruising we put into that firth, and anchored in the shelter of its hills.

There is no man of all our following who will forget that day, because of what happened almost as soon as the anchor held. It was very hot that morning, and what breeze had been out in the open sea was kept from us now by the hills, so that for some miles we had rowed the ships up the winding reaches of the firth; and then, as we laid in the oars and the anchorage was reached, there crept from inland a dim haze over the sun, dimming the light, and making all things look strange among the mountains. Then the sounds of the ships seemed to echo loudly over the still water and when all the bustle of anchoring was over, the stillness seemed yet greater, for the men went to their meals, and for a while spoke little.

Einar and I sat on his after deck under the awning, and spoke in low voices, as if afraid to raise our tones.

"There is a thunderstorm about," I said.

"Ay--listen," the jarl answered.

Then I heard among the hills, far up the firth beyond us, a strange sound that seemed to draw nearer, like and yet unlike thunder, roaring and jarring ever closer to us, till it was all around us and beneath us everywhere, and our very hearts seemed to stop beating in wonder.

Then of a sudden the ship was smitten from under the keel with a heavy, soundless blow, and the waters of the firth ebbed and flowed fiercely about us; and then the sound passed on and down the firth swiftly and strangely as it had come, and left us rocking on the troubled waters that plashed and broke along the rocks of the shore, while the still, thick air seemed full of the screams of the terrified eagles and sea birds that had left them.

"Odin defend us!" the jarl said; "what is this?"

I shook my head, looking at him, and wondering if my face was white and scared as his and that of every man whom I could see.

Now we waited breathless for more to come, but all was quiet again. The birds went back to their eyries, and the troubled water was still. Then presently our fears passed enough to let us speak with one another; and then there were voices enough, for every man wished to hear his own again, that courage might return.

Then a man from the Orkneys who had been with Jarl Sigurd came aft to us, and stood at the break of the deck to speak with Einar.

"Jarl," he said, almost under his breath, "it is in my mind that Sigurd, your brother, is wroth because his mound has been untended since we made it."

Then Einar said:

"Was it so ill made that it needs tending?"

"It was well made, jarl; but rain and frost and sun on a new-made mound may have wrought harm to it. Or maybe he thinks that enough honour has not been paid him. He was a great warrior, jarl, and perhaps would have more sacrifice, and a remembrance cup drunk by his own brother at his grave."

Now this man's name was Thord, the same who taught me runes--a good seaman and leader of men, and one who was held to be wise in more matters than most folk. So his word was to be listened to.

"You know more of these matters than I, Thord," Einar answered. "Is it possible that Sigurd could work this?"

"Who knows what a dead chief of might cannot work?" Thord said. "I think it certain that Sigurd is angry for some reason; and little luck shall we have if we do not appease his spirit."

Then the jarl looked troubled, as well he might, for to go near the mound that held an angry ghost was no light matter. It lay far up the firth, Thord said, and the ships could not go so far. But Einar was very brave, and when he had thought for a little while he said:

"Well, then, I will take boat and go to Sigurd's mound and see if he ails aught. Will any man come with me, however?"

I liked not the errand, as may be supposed, but I could not leave my foster father to go alone.

"I will be with you," I said. "Will not Thord come also?"

"Ay," the grim Orkney man answered.

Now all our crew were listening to us, and I looked down the long gangways by chance, and when I did so no man would meet my eye. They feared lest they should be made to go to this haunted place, as it seemed--all but one man, who sat on the mast step swinging his feet. This was Kolgrim the Tall, the captain of the fore deck, a young man and of few words, but a terrible swordsman, and knowing much of sea craft. And when this man saw that I looked at him, he nodded a little and smiled, for he had been a friend of mine since I had first come to Einar.

"Two men to row the boat will be enough, jarl," I said. "Kolgrim yonder will come with us."

"Well," the jarl answered, "maybe four of us are enough. We shall not fright Sigurd with more, and maybe would find it hard to get them to come."

So he called Kolgrim, and he said that he would go with us, and went to get the boat alongside without more words.

Then the jarl and I and Thord armed ourselves--for a warrior should be met by warriors. The men were very silent, whispering among themselves, until the jarl was ready and spoke to them.

"Have no fear for us," he said. "Doubtless my brother needs somewhat, and calls me. I am going to find out what it is and return."

So we pushed off, Thord and Kolgrim rowing. It was strange to look back, as we went, on the ships, for not a soul stirred on board them, as it seemed, so intently were we watched; and the water was like a sheet of steel under them, so that they were doubled.

Presently they were hidden as we rounded a turn in the firth, and we were alone among the hills, and the lonesomeness was very great. There was no dwelling anywhere along the shores, nor in the deep glens that came down to them, each with its noisy burn falling along it. Once I saw deer feeding far up at the head of a valley that opened out, but they and the eagles were the only living things we could see beside the loons that swam and dived silently as we neared them.

The silence and the heat weighed on us, and we went for a mile or more without a word. Then we turned into the last reach of the water, and saw Sigurd's mound beside its edge at the very head of the firth, where the hills came round in a circle that was broken only by the narrow waters and the valley that went beyond them among the mountains. It was a fitting resting place for one who would sleep in loneliness; but I thought that I had rather lie where I could look out on the sea I loved, and see the long ships pass and the white waves break beneath me.

Now all seemed very peaceful here in the hot haze that brooded over the still mountains, and there seemed to be nought to fear. We drew swiftly up to the mound, with the plash of oars only to break the silence, and there was nought amiss that we could see. They had made it on a little flat tongue of land that jutted from the mountain's foot into the deep water, so that on two sides the mound was close to its edge. So we pulled on softly round the tongue of land, being maybe about fifty paces from the mound across the water. And when we saw the other side of Sigurd's resting place, the oars stayed suddenly, and the jarl, who held the tiller, swung the boat away from the shore, and I think I knew then what fear was.

The mound was open. There was a wide, brown scar, as of freshly-moved earth, across its base, reaching from the level to six or eight feet of its height, as though half the grass-grown side had been shorn away by a sword cut; and in the midst of that scar was a doorway, open to the grave's heart, low and stone built. Some of the earth that had fallen lay before it on the water's edge, but the rest was doubtless in the water, for there was but a narrow path between bank and mound.

At that sight we stared, thinking we should surely see the grim form of Sigurd loom gigantic and troll-like across the doorway; and the jarl half rose from his seat beside me, and cried out with a great voice:

"Sigurd--my brother!"

I think he knew not what or why he cried thus, for he sank back into his place and swayed against me, while his cry rang loud among the hills, and the eagles answered it.

And I grasped my sword hilt, as one does in some sudden terror, staring at the open mound; while old Thord muttered spells against I know not what, and Kolgrim looked at me, pale and motionless.

Then came the sharp, mocking cry of a diver, that rang strangely; and at once, without order, Thord dug his oar blade into the water and swung the boat round, and when once Kolgrim's back was towards that he feared, he held water strongly and then the boat was about, and we were flying from the place towards the ships, before we knew what was being done, panic stricken.

But Einar said never a word, and the two rowers slackened their pace only when the bend of the firth hid the mound from our sight.

Then said I, finding that Einar spoke not:

"What are we flying from? there was nought to harm us."

For I began to be ashamed. Thereat Kolgrim stopped rowing, and Thord must needs do likewise, though he said:

"It is ill for us to stay here. The dead jarl is very wroth."

"I saw nought to fray us; the cry we heard was but that of a loon."

But Thord shook his head. The silence of the place had made all things seem strange, with the dull light that was over us, and the great heat among the towering hills.

"The mound was freshly opened," he said. "I saw earth crumbling even yet from the broken side. The blow we felt was that which Sigurd struck when he broke free."

Then at last Einar spoke, and his voice was strange:

"I have left my brother unhonoured, and he is angry. What must be done?"

Now I cannot tell what hardiness took hold of me, but it seemed that I must needs go back and see more of this. I was drawn to do so, as a thing they fear will make some men long to face it and know its worst, not as if they dared so much as when they must.

"I think we should have waited to ask Sigurd that," I said; and Einar looked strangely at me.

"Would you have us return?" he asked.

"Why not?" said I. "If the great jarl has called us as it seems, needs must that we know what he wills."

Then said Thord:

"I helped to lay him in that place, and I mind how he looked at that time. Somewhat we left undone, doubtless. I dare not go back."

Einar looked at the hills, leaning his chin on his hand, and said slowly, when Thord had done:

"That is the first time Thord has said 'I dare not.' Now I would that I had stayed to fight Harald and fall under his sword before. I too must say the same. I have left my brother unhonoured, and I dare not go back."

Pale and drawn the jarl's face was, and I knew he meant what he said. Nevertheless it seemed to me that some one must know what Sigurd willed.

"Jarl Einar," I said, "this is a strange business, and one cannot tell what it means. Now Sigurd was my father's close friend, and I have had nought to do with him. I will go back, therefore, and learn what I can of him. I think he will not harm me, for he has no reason to do so. Moreover if he does, none will learn what he needs."

"I have heard," said Thord, "that a good warrior may ask what he will of a dead hero, so that he shows no fear and is a friend. If his courage fails, however, then he will be surely destroyed."

Then I said:

"I have no cause to fear Sigurd, save that he is a ghost. I do not know if I fear him as such; that is to be seen."

Now Einar laid his hand on mine and spoke gravely:

"I think it is a hero's part to do what you say. If you go back and return in safety, the scalds will sing of you for many a long day. Go, therefore, boldly; this is not a matter from which you should be held back, as it has come into your mind."

Then said Thord:

"It will be well to ask Sigurd for a token whereby we may know that he sends messages by you."

And Einar said on that:

"In Sigurd's hand is his sword Helmbiter. I think he will give that to the man who dares speak to him, for he will know that it goes into brave hands. Ask him for it bravely."

"Put me ashore, therefore, before my courage goes," I said; and they pulled the boat to the bank where I could step on a rock and so to shore. And when I was there, Kolgrim rose up and followed me without a word.

"Bide here for two hours, jarl, and maybe I will return in that time," I said. "Farewell."

So I turned away as they answered me, thinking that Kolgrim held the boat's painter. But he came after me, and I spoke to him:

"Why, Kolgrim, will you come also?"

"You shall not go alone, Ranald the king's son; I will come with you as far as I dare."

"That is well," I answered, and with that wasted no more words, but climbed the hillside a little, and then went steadily towards where the mound was, with Kolgrim close at my shoulder, and the jarl and Thord looking fixedly after us till we were out of sight.

Chapter II. The Gifts of Two Heroes.

I will not say that my steps did not falter when we came to whence we could see the mound. But it was lonely and still and silent; no shape of warrior waited our coming.

"Almost do I fear to go nearer," said Kolgrim.

"Put fear away, comrade," said I; "we shall fare ill if we turn our backs now."

"Where you go I go," he answered, "though I am afraid."

"The next best thing to not being afraid is to be afraid and not to show it," I said then, comforting myself also with a show of wisdom at least. "Maybe fear is the worst thing we have to face."

So we went on more swiftly, and at last were on the tongue of land on the tip of which the mound stood. Still, since we could not see the open doorway, which was towards the water, the place seemed not so terrible. Yet I thought that by this time we should have seen Sigurd, or maybe heard his voice from the tomb. So now I dared to call softly:

"Jarl Sigurd, here is one, a friend's son, who will learn what you will."

My voice seemed to fill all the ring of mountains with echoes, but there was no answer. All was still again when the last voice came back from the hillsides.

Then I went nearer yet, and passed to the waterside, where I could look slantwise across the doorway. And again I called, and waited for an answer that did not come.

"It seems that I must go even to the door, and maybe into the mound," I said, whispering.

"Not inside," said Kolgrim, taking hold of my arm.

But I had grown bolder with the thought that the hero seemed not angry, and now I had set my heart on winning the sword of which the jarl had told me, and I thought that I dared go even inside the tomb to speak with Sigurd.

"Bide here, and I will go at least to the door," said I.

So I stepped boldly before it, standing on the heap of newly-fallen earth that had slipped from across it. The posts and lintel of the door were of stone slabs such as lay everywhere on the hillsides, and I stood so close that I could touch them. The doorway was not so high that I could see into it without stooping, for it was partly choked with the fallen earth, and I bent to look in. But I could only see for a few feet into the passage, as I looked from light to darkness.

"Ho, Jarl Sigurd! what would you? Why have you opened your door thus?"

Very hollow my voice sounded, and that was all.

"Sigurd of Orkney--Sigurd, son of Rognvald--I am the son of Vemund your friend. Speak to me!"

There was no answer. A bit of earth crumbled from the broken side of the mound and made me start, but I saw nothing. So I stepped away from the door and back to my comrade, who had edged nearer the place, though his face showed that he feared greatly.

"I think that the mound has been rifled," I said. "Sigurd would have us know it and take revenge."

"No man has dared to go near that doorway till you came, Ranald Vemundsson," Kolgrim answered. "Now I fear that he plans to lure you into the mound, and slay you there without light to help you. Go no further, maybe you will be closed up with the ghost."

That was not pleasant to think of, but I had seen nought to make me fear to go in. There was no such unearthly light shining within the mound as I had heard of in many tales of those who sought to speak with dead chiefs.

"Well, I am going in," I said stoutly; "but do you hide here, and make some noise that I may know you are near me. It is the silence that frays me.

"What can I do?" he said. "I know no runes that are of avail. It would be ill to disturb this place with idle sounds."

That seemed right, but I thought I could not bear the silence--silence of the grave. I must know that he was close at hand. Then a thought came to me, and I unfastened the silver-mounted whetstone that hung from my belt and gave it him.

"Whet your sword edge sharply," I said. "That is a sound a hero loves, for it speaks of deeds to be done."

"Ay, that is no idle sound," he said, and drew his sword gladly. The haft of the well-known blade brought the light into his eyes again. I drew my own sword also.

"If you need me, call, and I think I shall not fail you," he whispered. "It shall not be said that I failed you in peril."

"I know it," I answered, putting my hand on his shoulder.

Then I went boldly, and stepped into the passage. The whetstone sang shrill on the sword edge as it kissed the steel behind me, and the sound was good to hear as I went into darkness with my weapon ready.

I half feared that my first step would be my last, but it was made in safety. Very black seemed the low stone-walled passage before me, and I had to stoop as I went on, feeling with my left hand along the wall. The way was so narrow that little light could pass my body, and therefore it seemed to grow darker as I went deeper into the mound's heart.

Five steps I took, and then my outstretched hand was on the post that ended the passage, and beyond that I felt nothing. I had come to the inner doorway, and before me was the place where Sigurd lay. Yet no fiery eyes glared on me, and nothing stirred. The air was heavy with a scent as of peat, and the sound of the whetstone seemed loud as I stood peering into the darkness.

I moved forward, and somewhat rattled under my foot, and I started. Then my fear left me altogether, for I had trodden on dry bones, and shuddered at the first touch of them in that place. I had faced fear, and had overcome it; maybe it was desperation that made me cool then, for it was certain now that I must be slain or else victor over I knew not what.

So I took one pace forward into the chamber, and stood aside from the doorway; and the grey light from the passage came in and filled all the place, so that it fell first on him whom I had come to seek--Jarl Sigurd of Orkney.

And when I saw, a great awe fell upon me, and a sadness, but no terror; and in my heart I would that hereafter I might rest as slept the hero where the hands that had loved him had placed him.

Into the silent place came once more with me the clank of mail and weapons that he had loved, and from without the song of the keen sword edge whispered to him; but these could not wake him. Peacefully he seemed to sleep as I stood by his side, and I thought that I should take back no word of his to the jarl, his brother, whom both he and I loved.

They had brought the great carven chair on which he was wont to sit on his ship's quarterdeck, and thereon had set the jarl, as though he yet lived, and did but sleep as he sat from weariness after fight, with helm and mail upon him. Shield and axe rested on either side of him, ready to hand, against the chair; and behind him, along the wall, were his spears, ashen shafted and rune graven.

His blue, fur-trimmed cloak was round him, and before him was a little table, heavy and carved, whereon were vessels for food, empty now save for dust that showed that they had been full. And across his knees was his sword, golden hilted, with a great yellow cairngorm in the pommel, and with gold-wrought patterns from end to end of the scabbard--such a sword as I had never seen before. His right hand held the hilt, and his left rested on the shield's rim beside him; and so Sigurd slept with his head bowed on his breast, waiting for Ragnarock and the last great fight of all.

The light seemed to grow stronger as I looked, or my eyes grew used to it, and then I saw that the narrow chamber was full of things, though I minded them afterwards, for now I was as in a dream, noting only the jarl himself. Costly stuffs were on the floor, and mail and helms and more weapons. Gold work there was also, and in one corner lay the dried-up body of a great wolf hound, coiled as in sleep where it had been chained. Another had been tied by the passage doorway, where I had stepped on it; and below a spar that stood across a corner lay a tumbled heap of feathers that had been a falcon.

Many more things there were maybe, but this I saw at last--that the jarl's right foot rested on the skull of a man whose teeth had been long and tusk-like. It was the head of the Scot whose teeth had been his death.

Now the sword drew my eyes, for Einar bade me ask for it, else I think I had gone softly hence without a word, so peaceful seemed the dead. And as I looked again, I saw that the hand holding the hilt was dry and brown and shrunken, so that one might see all the bones through the skin, and at first I was afraid to ask.

At last I said, and my mouth was dry:

"Jarl Einar, your brother, bids me ask for sword Helmbiter, great Sigurd. Let me take it, that he may know how you rest in peace."

But Sigurd stirred not nor spoke; and slowly I put out my hand on the sword to take it very gently, but his grasp was yet firm on it. Then, as I bent to see if it had tightened when I would draw the sword away, I could see beneath the helm the face of the dead, shrunken indeed and brown, but as of one at rest and beyond anger.

Once more then I took the jarl's sword in my right hand, and raised his hand with my left, putting my own weapon by against the wall. And then the hilt slipped from the half-open fingers, and the sword was mine, and my hand held the jarl's. And it seemed to me that he gave it me, and that I must thank him for such a gift. The sword though it was sheathed, was not girt to him, and its golden-studded belt was twisted about it, and it was no imperfect giving.

So I spoke in a low voice:

"Jarl Sigurd, I thank you. If my might is aught, the sword will be used as you would have used it. Surely I will say to Einar that you rest in peace, and we will come here and close your mound again in all honour."

I set back his hand then, and it seemed empty and helpless, not as a warrior's should be. So I ungirt my own weapon--a good plain sword that I had won from a viking in Caithness--and laid it in the place of that he had given me. And as I put the thin fingers on its hilt, almost thinking that they would chose around it, a ring slipped from them into my hand, as if he would give that also, and I kept it therefore.

Then for a minute I stood before Jarl Sigurd, waiting to see if he had any word; but when he spoke not, I lifted the sword and saluted him.

"Skoal to Jarl Sigurd; rest in peace, and farewell."

Then I went forth softly, and came out into sunshine; for the wind was singing round the hilltops, and the dun mist had gone. Then I was ware that the sound of the stone on the sword edge had long ceased, and I looked for Kolgrim.

He was lying on the grass in the place where I had left him, but he was on his face, and the sword and whetstone were flung aside from him. At first I feared that he had been in some way slain because of his terror; but when I came near, I saw that his shoulders heaved as if he wept. Then I stood over him, treading softly.

"Kolgrim," I said.

At that he looked up, and a great light came into his face, and he sprang to his feet and threw his arms round me, weeping, yet with a strong man's weeping that does but come from bitter grief.

"Master," he cried, "O master I thought you lost--and I dared not follow you."

"I have met with no peril," I said, "nor have I been long gone."

"More than two hours, master, have you been in that place--two long hours. See how the sun has sunk since you left me!"

So indeed it seemed, though I knew not that I had been so long. I had stayed still and gazed on that strange sight without stirring for what seemed but a little while. Yet I had thought long thoughts in that time, and I mind every single thing in that dim chamber, even to the markings on the stones that made its walls and roof and floor.

"See," I said, "Jarl Sigurd has given me the sword!"

Kolgrim gazed in wonder. There was no speck of dust on the broad blade as I drew it, and the waving lines of the dwarf-wrought steel and gold-inlaid runes were clear and bright along its middle for half its length. For the mound was very dry, and they had covered all the chamber with peat before piling the earth over it.

"Let us go back to Jarl Einar; he will fear for us," I said, sheathing the sword and girding it to me.

So we went across the meadow, and even as we went a blast of cold wind came from, over the mountains, and with it whirled the black thunderclouds of the storm that had been gathering all day. We ran to an overhanging rock on the hillside and crept beneath it, while the thunder crashed and the lightning struck from side to side of the firth, and smote the wind-swept water that was white with foam.

"Master," said Kolgrim, "the Jarl Sigurd is wroth; he repents the sword gift."

But I did not think that he had aught to do with this. For, as any hill-bred man could tell, the storm had been brewing in the heat, and was bound to come, and would pass to and fro among the hills till it was worn out.

Nevertheless, when it passed away in pouring rain that swept like a hanging sheet of moving mist down the glens from the half-hidden mountains, and the sun shone out brightly again over the clear-cut purple hillsides and rippling water, I looked at the mound in wonder. For it was closed. We had sought shelter in a place near that whence we saw the mound in coming, and could see the fallen side, though not the doorway, looking across its front. And now the slope of the bank seemed to have been made afresh, as on the day when Sigurd had been closed in, years ago. None could say, save those who had seen it, where the opening into the grave-chamber might be.

Now both the opening and closing of Sigurd's grave mound seem very strange to me. Thord and the scalds will have it that he himself wrought both. As for me, I know not. In after days I told this to Alfred the king when he wondered at my sword, and he said that he thought an earthquake opened and washing rain closed the mound, but that it happened strangely for me. I cannot gainsay his wise words, and I will leave the matter so.

Thereafter Kolgrim and I went back to Einar, who yet waited for us. Glad was he to see us return in safety; but both he and Thord were speechless when they saw the jarl's sword girt to me and the jarl's golden ring on my hand. Neither they nor any one else will believe that I met with no peril; and the tale that the scalds made hereafter of the matter is over wonderful, in spite of all I may say. For they think it but right that I should not be over boastful of my deeds.

But Jarl Einar looked on sword and ring, and said:

"Well have you won these gifts. My brother is in peace in his resting place now. I hold that he called for you."

So we went back to the ships, and there for many days the men stared at Kolgrim and me strangely. They say I was very silent for long, and it is likely enough. Moreover, Einar was wont to say that I seemed five years older from that day forward.

We went no more to the place of the mound, for it seemed to need no care of earthly hands. Nor were any wishing to go to so awesome a place, and we left the firth next day, for the men waxed uneasy there.

But on that day Einar gave me the great ship that we had taken from Halfdan, the king's son, saying that he would add to Sigurd's giving. Also he bade me choose what men I would for her crew, bidding me thank him not at all, for I was his foster son, and a king by birth moreover.

So when I knew that this would please him, I chose Thord for my shipmaster, and Kolgrim for marshal, as we call the one who has charge of the ordering of the crew. And I chose a hundred good men whom I knew well, so that indeed I had the best ship and following in Norway, as I thought. At least there were none better, unless Harald Fairhair might match me.

Now there was one thing that pleased me not at this time, and that was that Kolgrim, my comrade, never called me aught but "master" since I came from Sigurd's presence--which is not the wont of our free Norsemen with any man. Nor would he change it, though I was angry, until I grew used to it in time.

"Call me not 'master,' Kolgrim, my comrade," I said; "it is unfitting for you."

At last he answered me in such wise that I knew it was of no more use to speak of it.

"Master of mine you are, Ranald the king, since the day when you dared more than I thought man might, while I lay like a beaten hound outside, and dared not go within that place to see what had become of you. Little comradeship was mine to you on that day, and I am minded to make amends if I can. I think I may dare aught against living men for you, though I failed at that mound. I will give life for you, if I may."

I told him that what he had done was well done, and indeed he had had courage to go where none else had dared; for I had ties of friendship that made me bold to meet Jarl Sigurd, and might go therefore where he might not. It was well that he did not come into the presence of the dead.

"Therefore we are comrades, not master and man," I said.

"Nay, but master and man--lord and thrall," he answered.

So I must let him have his way, but he could not make me think of him as aught but a good and brave comrade whom I loved well.

They hailed me as king when I went on board my ship for the first time with my own men, as I have said. Then our best weapon smith asked for gold from the men, and they gave what they had--it was in plenty with us of Einar's following--and made a golden circlet round my helm, that they might see it and follow it in battle.

It was good to wear the crown thus given willingly, but in the end it sent me from north to south, as will be seen. That, however, is a matter with which I will not quarrel, for it sent me to Alfred the king.

We had left the firth two days, cruising slowly northward, when one ship came from the north and met us, not flying from our fleet, but bearing up to join us. And when she was close, there came a hail to tell Einar that she bore a messenger from Harald the king in peace, and presently we hove to while this messenger went on board the Jarl's ship.

Then it seemed that Einar had been right, and that Harald would lay a fine on the islands for Halfdan's slaying, and so give them back to Einar to hold for him. The messenger was Thiodolf, Harald's own scald, and he put the matter very plainly before the jarl, so that he thought well of the offer, but would nevertheless not trust himself in the king's power before all was certain, and confirmed by oath. Whereon Thiodolf said that one must see the king on the Jarl's part, and so I seemed the right man to go, as the jarl's foster son and next in command to him.

"Nevertheless," said Thiodolf, "I would not advise you to sail in Halfdan's ship, for that might wake angry thoughts, and trouble would come especially as Halfdan took her without leave when he was outlawed."

So I took the Jarl's cutter, manning her with enough men of my own crew; and Kolgrim came with me, and we sailed to Kirkwall in company with Thiodolf the scald.

Then when Thiodolf took me into his presence, I saw Harald Fairhair for the first time, as he sat to receive Einar's messenger in the great hall that Sigurd had built and which we had dwelt in. Then I thought that never before could have been one more like a king. Hereafter, when sagamen will sing of a king in some fancied story, they will surely make him like King Harald of Norway. I myself have little skill to say what he was like beyond this--that never had I seen a more handsome man, nor bigger, nor stronger. King-like he was in all ways, and his face was bright and pleasant, though it was plain that it would be terrible if he was angry, or with the light of battle upon it.

The hair, whence he had his name, was golden bright and shining, and beard and eyebrows were of the same colour. But his eyes were neither grey nor blue altogether, most piercing, seeming to look straight into a man's heart, so that none dared lie to him.

I think that it is saying much for King Harald that, though his arms and dress were wonderfully rich and splendid, one cared only to look on his face; and that though many men of worth were on the high place with him, there seemed to be none but he present.

When the scald told the king who I was, and what was my errand, with all ceremony, he looked fixedly at me, so that I was ashamed, and grew red under his gaze. Then he smiled pleasantly, and spoke to me. His voice was as I thought to hear it--clear and steady, and yet deep.

"So, Ranald Vemundsson, you are worthy of your father. It may be that you bear me ill will on his account, but I would have you forget the deeds done that Norway might be one, and the happier therefor."

"Had my father been slain in fair fight, lord king," I said, "no ill will had been thought of. It has not been in my mind that you bade Rognvald slay him as he did. And that Jarl is dead, and the feud is done with therefore. Jarl Einar is my foster father, moreover."

"That is well said," answered Harald. "But I thought Sigurd must have fostered you; he was ever a close friend of Vemund's."

I did not know why the king thought this, though the reason was at my side; so I only said that my mother had given me to Einar's keeping, and the king said no more at that time about it.

After that I gave the Jarl's messages, and the king heard them well enough, though it seemed to Einar that the weregild to be paid was over heavy, and he had bidden me tell Harald that it was so. Therefore the king said that he would give me an answer on the morrow, and I went away into the town well pleased with his kindly way with me.

There was a feast made for me that night, and after it I must sit still and hear the scalds sing of the deeds of Harald the king, which was well enough. But then Thiodolf rose up and sang a great saga about the winning of Sigurd's sword, wherein it seemed that I had fought the dead jarl, and bale fires, and I know not what. He had heard strange tales from Einar's men, if they told him all that he sang.

Some men may be pleased to hear their own deeds sung of, with more added thus; but I was not used to it, and the turning of all eyes to me made me uncomfortable. But Harald had paid no sort of heed to what they sang of him, and so I tried to look at my ease, and gave the scald a bracelet when he ended.

"Overmuch make you of that matter, scald," said I quietly.

He laughed a little, and answered:

"One has to fill in what a warrior will not tell of himself."

Now the men shouted when I gave Thiodolf the bracelet, and Harald looked quickly at me. Then I thought that maybe I had overdone the gift, though Einar had ever told me that a good scald deserved good reward, and Thiodolf was well known as the best in Norway. It was a heavy ring, silver gilt, and of good design, that I took from the same viking whose sword I gave to Sigurd.

"Overpaid am I," the scald said, putting it on his arm.

"You are the first who has ever sung of me," I answered; "and the voice and tune were wonderful, if the saga was too strong for me."

Then Harald smiled again, and praised Thiodolf also, and I thought no more of the matter. The feast was pleasant enough in the hall, full of Harald's best men and chiefs, though it seemed strange to sit as a guest in Einar's house.

Now on the next morning I was to speak with the king about Einar's business, and I went to him unarmed, as was right, save for helm and Sigurd's sword. He was in the jarl's own chamber, and with him were Thiodolf and a young scald named Harek, who sat with things for writing before him, which was what I had never seen before.

We talked for some time, and all went well for peace; but one more message was to go and come between the king and Einar, and so I said I would sail at once.

"Not so much need for haste but that you can bide here for a day or two," Harald said. "I will not have you complain of my hospitality hereafter. And Thiodolf and Harek here want to learn more about Sigurd's sword and its winning."

"If I tell them the truth, I shall spoil their saga, lord king!" I said, laughing.

"Trust the scalds to mind you do not," he answered. "There are times when I have to ask them which of my own doings they are singing about now. But is there no wonder in the tale?"

So I told him just how the matter was. And when he heard of the noise, and the stroke with which the ships were smitten, he said, looking troubled, as I thought:

"Sigurd is stronger now that he is dead than when he lived. We felt that stroke even here."

But when I told how I had seen the dead jarl, his face grew thoughtful, and at last he said:

"So shall I lie some day in a grave mound. It is passing strange to think on. I would that if one comes to my side he may step gently as you, Ranald Vemundsson."

"Else will that comer fare ill," said Thiodolf.

The king glanced up at him, and his face changed, and he said, smiling grimly:

"Maybe. I think none will win my sword from me."

Then he had Kolgrim sent for, and Thord, and they told him truly what they had seen, and how they had fared in the matter.

"You are a truth teller, Kolgrim the Tall," Harald said. "Now if you will leave Einar's service and come and be of my courtmen, I will speak to the jarl and make matters right with him, and it shall be worth your while."

Then my comrade answered plainly:

"I am no jarl's man now, King Harald; I belong to King Ranald here, and I will not leave him."

"So," said Harald, knitting his brows suddenly, "we have two kings in the room, as it seems; and you dare choose another instead of me."

"Not so, King Harald," Kolgrim answered, with all respect; "I chose between the jarl and my king. If there is peace between you and the jarl, I suppose we are all your men."

Now Harald's face was growing black, and I could see that his anger was rising. But he stayed what words he was about to speak, and only said:

"Jarl Einar is well served when he has a king in his train."

Then he rose up and turned to Thiodolf, who was looking anxious.

"Bid King Ranald to the feast tonight. He knows my words to Einar his foster father, and I have no more to say."

So I was dismissed, and was not sorry to be outside the hall.

"Let us get down to the ship," said Thord. "Here is trouble brewing, as I think."

So we went on board, and I wished that we might go. Yet the king had bidden me stay, and I had no reason for what would be discourteous at least, if it did not look like flight. What the trouble was we could hardly understand.

In an hour's time or so I saw Thiodolf and the young scald Harek coming along the wharf and towards our ship, which lay clear of Harald's vessels, and next the harbour mouth. They came over the gang plank, and I welcomed them, but I saw that they had somewhat special to say to me.

They sat down under the after awning with me, and at once Thiodolf said:

"That was an unlucky speech of your comrade's just now. No man dares name himself king in Harald's presence--not even his own sons. It is the one thing that he will not bear."

"So it seemed," said I; "and, in truth, he had enough trouble with under kings not long since. But he knows what a sea king is--no king at all, so to speak. He need not grudge the old title."

"That is not all," Thiodolf said. "It is in his mind that he has to guard yet against risings of men of the old families of the kings, and thinks you are likely to give him trouble. Maybe the portent of the blow that spread from Sigurd's tomb to us has seemed much to him. 'Here,' he says, 'is one who will gather masterless men to him in crowds because he wears Sigurd's sword and ring, and has gained with them the name of a hero. Already he has two of Einar's best men at his heels. Yet I like him well enough, and I have no fault to find with him, save that he puts a gold circle round his helm and is called king--as he would have been but for me. Go to him, therefore, and tell him to keep out of my way. I will not have two kings in Norway.'"

"Well," I said, "that is plain speaking. But I cannot help what the men call me. The king makes overmuch of the business. I am not foolish enough to try to overturn Harald Fairhair."

"Maybe," said Thiodolf, "but those are his words. I rede you get away quickly on the next tide."

"Ay," said Harek. "Harald is mild of mood now, because you made no secret of what men call you. Five years ago you would not have escaped hence at all."

"Then," said I, "I will go. I think you are right. Vemund's son troubles Harald;" and I laughed, and added, "I have to thank you for kindly counsel, scalds, as I think. Farewell. Tide serves at any time now, and I will get my men and be gone."

"That is wise," they answered. "Einar must find some other messenger, if he comes not himself, after you return."

They went, and I called two or three men and sent them into the town for their comrades who were at friends' houses and in the guest house where we were lodged, while Kolgrim made ready for instant sailing.

The next thing that I was ware of was that there was a fight on the wharf end next the town, and men were running to it. Then I heard my own name shouted on one part, and that of Eric, the king's young son, on the other. So I was going to lead down twenty men to quiet the scuffle, when my people had the best of the matter, and broke through the throng, cheering, and came on to me. The rest did not follow them, for they saw that I was coming, and the wharf was clear behind them but for three of their foes who stayed where they had fallen.

Then another man broke away from the crowd, and came running after my folk. It was Harek the scald, with his head broken.

"Here are fine doings," said Kolgrim, as the men swarmed on board. "What is on hand now?"

"It is not done with yet," said a man: "look at yon ship."

Then came Harek, out of breath, and pale.

"Let me on board, King Ranald, or I am a dead man," he cried.

"Come, then!" I answered; and he ran across the plank, and Kolgrim pulled it in after him. All my men were come.

Then I looked at the ship spoken of. Men were swarming into her, and were making ready to sail. But if she meant to stay our going, she was too far up the harbour, and we were already casting off the shore ropes.

"Hold on," said Thord; "here come the other scald and two men."

The crowd that was yet round the fallen men had parted to let Thiodolf pass, and he came quickly. One of the men bore a chest, and the other a bale of somewhat. They gave these over the gunwale to my people, and Thiodolf spoke to me from the wharf.

"These are gifts from Harald to Einar's foster son," he said. "He bids me say that you have done your errand well, and that this is to prove it. Also he says that Ranald, son of Vemund, may need mail to keep his kingship withal, and so he has sent you a suit."

"That is a hard saying," I answered; "is it insult?"

"Nay, but a broad hint only. The gift is most goodly."

"Well," said I, "it is plain that he will warn me from Norway. I will leave you, good friend, to say for me what should be said. Maybe if I sent a message it would go wrongly from my lips."

Thiodolf laughed, and bade me farewell. He paid no heed to Harek, who sat on the deck with his back to him.

Then Kolgrim whistled shrill to his men, and we began to move down to the harbour mouth. I heard a sharp voice hurrying the men in the other ship; but they could not be ready in time to catch us.

When we were well out to sea, I asked Harek what all this was about.

"Your going has spoiled a plan that Eric, the king's son, had made. He wanted your sword, and thought also that to rid himself now of Vemund's son might save him trouble when the crown came to him, as it will. You were to be set on as you came from the feast tonight to the guest quarters, as if in a common broil between your men and his. Then he found you were going, and tried to stay your men, and next to take these gifts from Thiodolf and me, being very angry, even to trying to cut me down. Lucky for me that his sword turned in his hand. But he would have had me slain tonight, certainly, for he says that it was our fault that you are getting away. He fears Thiodolf, however. Now I must take service with you, if you will have me."

It seemed to me that I was making friends with one hand and enemies with the other, and that last rather more quickly than was well. So I laughed, and answered:

"I suppose that if I have a scald of my own, King Harald will blame me for overmuch kingship. However, he is angry enough already, and maybe a good friend will balance that to me. So if you will indeed cast in your lot with me, I am glad!"

So I took his hand, and more than friends have he and I been from that day forward.

Now, when I looked at Harald's strangely-given gifts, I had reason to say that he was open handed. The chest held two mail shirts, one of steel rings, gold ornamented and fastened, and the other of scales on deerskin, both fit for a king. There were two helms also, one to match either byrnie [liv], and a seax that was fit to hang with Sigurd's sword. As for the bale, that held furs of the best, and blue cloth and scarlet. If Harald banished me, it was for no ill will; and it was handsomely done, as though he would fit me out for the viking's path in all honour, that men might not deem me outlawed for wrongdoing. So I have no ill word to say against him. Five years later he would have troubled about me and my kingship not at all; now he must be careful, for his power was not at its full.

As for young Eric, I suppose that he boasted ever after that he had put me to flight; but I do not know that it matters if he did.

So I came back to Durness, where I was to meet with Einar; and peace was made between him and the king, and he thought it well to go and speak with him. Then he and I must part, and that was hard.

"Now must you go your own way, son Ranald, for Harald is too strong for us. Maybe that is best for you, for here shall I bide in peace in Orkney; and that is not a life for a king's son--to sit at a jarl's table in idleness, or fight petty fights for scatt withholden and the like. Better for you the wide seas and the lands where you may make a name, and maybe a kingdom, for yourself. Yet I shall miss you sorely."

So he said, and I knew that he was right. Maybe the spirit of the sword I had won got hold of me, as they say will happen; for I had waxed restless of late, and I had tried to keep it from Einar. Now I hated myself for it, seeing at hand what I had longed for.

So he went north to meet Harald, and of our parting I will not say more. I could not then tell that I should not see him again, and that was well: but I know that when I saw the last flicker of his sails against the sky, I felt more lonely even than at the graveside in Southmere.

Yet I was in no worse case than were many nobly-born men at that time; for whosoever would not bow to Harald and his new laws must leave Norway, and her bravest were seeking new homes everywhere. Some had gone to far-off Iceland, and some to East Anglia; some to the Greek emperor, or Gardariki, and more yet to Ireland. But the greatest viking of all, Rolf, the son of Rognvald, Einar's young brother, had gone to France or England, with a mighty following; for Harald had outlawed him among the first who broke his law by plundering on the Norway coasts. A good law it was, but it was new, and so went against the grain at first. Rolf had sworn to make a new kingdom for himself, and why should not I do the same?

So when I was in the open sea again, with all the world before me, as the long sea-miles passed I grew lighthearted, and many were the thoughts of great deeds to come that filled my mind.

Chapter III. Odda, the Ealdorman of Devon.

Now I steered eastward from Sutherland, and sailed down the east coasts of Scotland and England; and there is nothing to say about such a cruise, that had nought more wonderful in it than the scaring of the folk when we put in for food. I had made up my mind to go to Ireland for the winter, where, as every Northman knew, there were kingdoms to be won--having no wish to be Rolf's follower, seeing he was but a jarl's son; and finding that England had no overlord, seeing that even now Alfred of Wessex and Guthrum of East Anglia were fighting for mastery, so that the whole land was racked and torn with strife.

Maybe I thought too much of myself at that time, but I was in no haste to do aught but cruise about and find where I might best make a name. I had but my one ship and crew, and I would not throw them away on some useless business for want of care in choosing.

Now, when we came into the English Channel, a gale began to blow up from the southwest; and we held over to the French shore, and there put into a haven that was sheltered enough. The gale strengthened, and lasted three days; but the people were kindly enough, being of Saxon kin, who had settled there under the headland they call Greynose, since Hengist's times of the winning of England across the water. And when the gale was over, we waited for the sea to go down, and then came a fair wind from the eastward, as we expected. So we got provisions on board, and sailed westward again, taking a long slant over to the English coast, until we sighted the great rock of Portland; and then the wind came off the land, and in the early morning veered to the northwest.

The tide was still with us as the light strengthened; then as the day broke, with the haze of late summer over the land, we found that we were right in the track of a strange fleet that was coming up fast from the westward--great ships and small, in a strange medley and in no sort of order, so that we wondered what they would be.

"Here comes Rolf Ganger back from Valland," said Kolgrim. "He has gathered any vessels he could get together, and is going to land in England."

"We will even head out to sea from across their course," I said. "Maybe they are Danes from Exeter, flying from the Saxons."

So we headed away for the open channel until at least we knew more. The fleet drew up steadily, bringing the tide with them; and presently we fell to wondering at the gathering. For there were some half-dozen ships that were plainly Norse like ourselves, maybe twenty Danish-built longships, and about the same number of heavy trading vessels. There were a few large fishing boats also; but leading the crowd were five great vessels the like of which none of us had ever seen or heard of before. And even as we spoke of them, two of these shook out reefs in their sails, and drew away from the rest across channel, as if to cut us off.

"Ho, men," I said, when I saw that, "get to arms; for here they come to speak with us. Maybe we shall have to fight--and these are no easy nuts to crack!"

Whereat the men laughed; and straightway there was the pleasant hustle and talk of those who donned mail shirt and helm and set the throwing weapons to hand with all good will.

"Let us keep on our course," I said to Kolgrim. "We will see if we cannot weather on these ships, and anyway shall fight them better apart from the rest. It is a fine breeze for a sailing match."

So we held on; and the two great ships to windward of us began to gain on us slowly, which was a thing that had never been done by any ship before. I do not know that even Harald Fairhair had any swifter ship than this that Halfdan had taken in his flight from home. Kolgrim waxed very wroth when it became plain that these could outsail us.

"There is witchcraft about those great hulks," he growled. "They are neither Norse, nor Frisian, nor Danish, but better than all three put together."

"I have sailed in ships, and talked of ships, and dreamed of them moreover, since I could stand alone," said Thord, "but I never so much as thought of the like of these. If they belong to some new kind of viking, there are hard times in store for some of us."

"Faith," said I, "I believe they have swept up and made prizes of all that medley astern of them."

So we held on for half an hour, and all that time they gained steadily on us; and we neared them quickly at last, for we tried to hold across their bows and weather on them. That was no good, for they were as weatherly as we.

Now we could see that their decks were covered with armed men, and it seemed certain that they meant to make prize of us. The leading ship was maybe half a mile ahead of the other, and that a mile from us--all three close-hauled as we strove to gain a weather berth. Then the leading ship put her helm up and stood across our course, and the second followed her.

"We must out oars now if we are to weather on them," said Kolgrim at last.

Then the men shouted; and I looked at the second ship, to which they were pointing. Her great sail was overboard, for the halliards had gone--chafed through maybe, or snapped with the strain as she paid off quickly. Then a new hope came to me.

"Men," I said, "let us take the other vessel, and then come back on this; they are worth winning."

They cheered. And now the fight seemed to be even--ship to ship at least, if our foe was larger and higher and swifter than ours; for I thought that he would hardly have a crew like mine.

We up helm and stood away on the new course the foe had taken, leaving the crippled ship astern very fast. And now we began to edge up towards the other vessel, meaning to go about under her stern, and so shoot to windward of her on the other tack. But then I thought of a plan which might help us in the fighting. There had seemed little order and much shouting on board the ship we had left when her sail fell, and maybe there was the same want of discipline here.

"Out oars, men! Keep them swinging, but put no weight on them. Let them pull after us and tire themselves. I have a mind to see how our dragon looks on yonder high stem head."

The men laughed grimly, and the oars were run out. One called to me:

"Maybe they beat us in sailing, king; we can teach them somewhat in weapon play."

"See how they get their oars out," said Kolgrim, with a sour grin; "a set of lubbers they are."

One by one, and in no order, the long oars were being got to work. The great ship was half as long again as ours, pulling twenty-eight oars a side to our twenty. But while ours rose and fell as if worked by one man, theirs were pulled anyhow, as one might say.

"Better are they at sailing than rowing," said Thord.

Nevertheless they flew down on us, and that because we only made a show of rowing.

Then we laid on the oars, and came head to wind. The sail rattled down, and was stowed on deck; and silently we waited, arrows on string, for the fight that was now close at hand.

Then the great ship hove up, head to wind, right ahead of us, and a loud hail came from her.

"Who knows what tongue he talks?" I said. "I cannot make him out rightly."

"'Tis West Saxon," said an old warrior from the waist. "He asks who we are and what is our business."

"Tell him therefore, if you can speak in his way," I answered; "and ask the same of him."

So a hail or two went backwards and forwards, and then:

"Says he is Odda, jarl or somewhat of Devon in Wessex, and bids us yield to Alfred the king."

"In truth," said I, "if he had not spoken of yielding, I had had more to say to a king who can build ships like these. Now we will speak with him on his own deck. Tell him he will have to fight us first."

The old warrior sent a mighty curt hail back in answer to Odda's summons; then our war horns blew, and the oars rose and fell, and we were grinding our bows alongside the great ship's quarter before they knew we were there. Alfred's men had yet somewhat to learn of fighting in a sea way, as it seemed, for we were on their deck aft before they had risen from their oar benches. There were but one or two men on the quarter deck, besides the steersman, to oppose us. Odda thought we should lay our ship alongside his towering sides if we fought, as I suppose, for he was amidships.

So we swept the decks from aft forward without any hurt to ourselves: for the Saxons were hampered with the oars, and fell backward over them, and hindered one another. It was strange to hear my men laughing in what seemed most terrible slaughter; for their foes fell before they were smitten, and lay helpless under the oars, while their comrades fell over them.

So we won to the foot of the mast, and then found that there were some on board who were none so helpless: for as we came they swung the great yard athwart ships, and that stayed us; while over the heap of canvas glared those who would make it hard for us to win the ship altogether.

But before we came to stern fighting, I had a word to say; so I called for Odda.

A square built, brown-bearded man with a red, angry face pushed his way to the front of his men, and frowned at me.

"What will you? here am I," he said shortly.

One could understand his words well enough when face to face, for he spoke in the mixed tongue that any Northman understands, the plain words of which all our kin have in common.

"I am no foe of Alfred's," I said; "I do not know, therefore, why I should fight you."

"Are you not for the Danes?" he said.

"I hate them more or less, and I have no traffic with them."

"Well, then, what will you?"

"You bade me yield, and therefore I am here. Now I think it is a matter to be seen whether of us does so."

"It seems that you have slain about half my men," he said. "Nevertheless, I do not give up without fighting for the rest of my ship that you have not won."

"That is well said," I answered.

But the men were laughing, for Kolgrim had stooped, and, reaching under an oar bench, had dragged out a rower by the neck. The man swore and struggled; but Kolgrim hove him up, and lifted him over the yard to Odda's feet.

"They are all like that, Saxon," he said cheerfully. "Maybe there is a head or two broken; 'tis mostly what we call seasickness, however."

Odda looked at the man, who seemed wretched enough, but had no hurt; then he stared at our laughing faces, and his own brow began to clear.

"It comes into my mind," he said, "that maybe you would listen to me if I owned first that you have the best of us, and then asked you to fight for Alfred of Wessex. We need the help of such men as you just now; and if you hate Danes, we have work enough for you."

"One may certainly listen to that," I answered, laughing.

"What say you, men? Shall we cast in our lot with Alfred for a while?"

"We follow you, Ranald the king," Kolgrim answered for all. "If it seems good to you, it is good for us. There will be fighting enough, I trow, if all we have heard is true."

Then said Odda:

"And that before long. There is a Danish fleet in Poole Harbour that is to bring Danes from Wareham to the help of those whom Alfred holds in Exeter. We have to meet this fleet and scatter it."

"Then," said old Thord, "your men must be better handled, for Danes are no new swordsmen or seamen either."

Now the men stood listening to our talk, and this sort of saying was not good for them to hear, if they were to meet the foe soon with a good hope of victory. So Odda said quickly:

"If you will indeed fight for us, you must trust to Alfred to give you fitting reward. I do not know what I might say about that, having thought of no such chance as this. But there is no man who can complain of him."

I had heard that the king was ever open handed, but also that at this time he had little to give. Maybe, however, we might help him to riches again. I had the men to think of, but I will say for myself that I had not thought of asking what reward or pay should be given.

I sheathed my sword, and held out my hand to Odda across the yard that was between us; and he grasped it honestly, while the men on either side cheered.

"Stay here and speak with me," Odda said. "Now we must get back to the fleet."

Then went back to our ship, all but Thord and half a dozen warriors, whom he kept as guard for me, I suppose; and the grappling lines were cast off. Then we made sail again, and headed to rejoin the rest of the Saxon vessels. Odda's crippled ship had repaired her damage at this time, and went with us. But first it was plain that she thought we had taken her consort, for she prepared to fight us, and Odda had to hail her once or twice before she was sure of what had happened. Then her crew cheered also.

Now Odda took me aft, and we sat together on his quarter deck. Thord came also, and leaned on the rail beside us, looking with much disfavour at the crew, who were plainly landsmen at sea for the first time, if they were stout fighting men enough. Maybe there were ten seamen among the hundred and fifty, but these had handled the ship well under canvas, as we knew.

"You have come in good time, King Ranald," Odda said. "You see what state we are in; can you better it for us?"

"Many things I can see that need strengthening," I answered. "But you seem to take me into your counsels over soon, seeing that I have just fallen on you sword in hand."

"Why," said Odda frankly, "it is just your way of speaking to me sword in hand that makes me sure that I can trust you. I cannot deny that you had this ship at your mercy, and that the other would have been yours next; and you knew it, and yet spoke me fair. So it is plain that you mean well by us."

"Ay," said I, "but for your bidding me to yield, there would have been no fighting at all, when I knew to whom the ships belonged."

"You have put a thought in my mind, and I am glad you did board us, seeing there is no harm done," Odda answered. "I will tell you what it is. Send me some of your men to order my people and tell them how to prepare for battle. Here am I sent to sea for the first time, with good warriors enough who are in like case, and a few seamen who can sail the ship and know nought else."

"You have some Norsemen yonder, if I mistake not," I said, looking at the fleet which we were nearing.

"Ay--wandering vikings who care nought for what I say. They were going to Rolf, and the king persuaded them to take this cruise first. If you can make them follow you, there will be another matter for which I shall be more than thankful."

Thereat Thord growled: "They will follow Ranald Vemundsson well enough; have no care about that."

Then said I:

"These are the finest ships I have ever seen. Where did they come from?"

"Alfred, our king, planned them," said Odda, with much pride; "and they were built by our own men, working under Frisian shipwrights, in Plymouth."

"How will you like to command one of these, Thord?" I asked then.

"I like the ship well enough. The crew is bad. And then, whose command is the fleet under?"

"Take the ship, Thord, and lick my crew into shape; and Ranald, your king, shall command the fleet," Odda said plainly.

"Fair and softly," said Thord bluntly. "I can do the two things you ask me; but will your men follow Ranald?"

"Faith," said Odda, "if I say they are to do so, they must."

So in the end I left Thord and my seamen with Odda; but I would not take his place, only saying that I would lead the Norsemen, and that he could follow our plans. I would put more good men into each of his five ships, and they should do what they could. At least they could teach the Saxons how to board a ship, and how to man their own sides against boarders from a foe.

Those Norsemen said they would gladly follow the son of King Vernund and foster son of Einar the jarl; and so we led the strange fleet, and held on eastward with a light breeze all that day, making little way when the tide turned, and held back by the slower vessels. Men in plenty there were, but ill fitted for aught but hand fighting; though I had more Norsemen sent into the larger ships, such as those that had been taken from the Danes and the better trading vessels. One might soon see the difference in the trim and order on board as the vikings got to work and the Saxons overcame their sickness.

Now we might meet the Danes at any time, and I could not tell how matters would go. One thing was certain, however, and that was that they looked for no gathering of ships by Alfred. We should certainly take them by surprise, and I hoped, therefore, that they would be in no trim for fighting.

There was a very swift cutter belonging to the Norsemen, and as night fell I sent her on to keep watch along the shore for the first coming of the Danes, while we shortened sail; for the mouth of Poole Harbour was not far distant, and if we passed that we should be seen, and perhaps it would be guessed that we were not a friendly fleet. Towards evening, too, the wind shifted, and blew more off the shore, and that might bring them out from their haven. Kolgrim, who was weather wise, said that a shift of wind to the southward was coming presently.

When morning came, the high cliffs of Swanage were on our bow, the wind was yet steady from off shore, and beyond the headland lay Poole Harbour, at whose head is Wareham, where the Danes were. It is a great sea inlet with a narrow mouth, and one must have water enough on a rising tide to enter it. Now the ebb was running, and if the Danes came this morning, it would be soon.

They came, as it seemed, for the cutter was flying back to us under sail and oars; and before she reached us, the first Danish ships were clear of the Swanage headlands, making for the offing. Then I got my ships into line abreast, and Thord worked up Odda's five alongside us to seaward; and all the while the Danish sails hove into sight in no sort of order, and seeming so sure that none but friends could be afloat that they paid no heed to us.

Soon there were full a hundred vessels of all sorts off Swanage point, and the cutter brought word that there were but twenty more. Then I ran up my fighting flag, and everywhere along our line rose a great cheering as we hoisted sail and sped down on the foe. It was long since the seas had borne a fleet whence the Saxon war cry rang.

The leading Danes were ahead of us as we gathered way, and their long line straggled right athwart our course. We should strike their midmost ships; and at last they saw what was coming, and heard the din of war horns and men's voices that came down wind to them, and there were confusion and clamour on their decks, and voices seemed to call for order that did not come.

Then one or two longships from among them struck sail and cleared for action, and on these swooped Alfred's great ships. Odda's crashed upon and sank the first she met, and plunged and shook herself free from the wreck, and sought another. And beyond her the same was being wrought; and cheers and cries were strangely mixed where those high bows went forward unfaltering.

Now a ship crowded with men was before me. As we boarded, her crew were yet half armed, and struggling to reach the weapon chests through the press, even while our dragon head was splintering the gunwale; and I leaped on board her, with my men after me and Harek beside me.

Then sword Helmbiter was let loose for the first time since Sigurd wielded her; and though a great and terrible cry came from over the water as one of Alfred's ships sank another Dane, I could look no more, for there was stern fighting before me.

What a sword that was! Hardly could my arm feel the weight of it as it swung in perfect balance, and yet I knew the weight it had as it fell. Helm and mail seemed as nought before the keen edge, and the shields flew in twain as it touched them.

Forward I went, and aft went Harek the scald, and there was soon an end. The Danes went overboard, swimming or sinking, as their fate might be, and only the slain bided before us. The ship was ours, and I looked round to see what should be next. No other ship had come to help our prey.

Then I saw a wonderful sight. Panic terror had fallen on the Danes, and not one ship of all that great fleet was not flying down the wind without thought of fighting. Among them went our vessels, great and small, each doing her work well; and the Saxon shouts were full of victory.

So we must after them, and once more we boarded a longship, and had the victory; and then we were off the haven mouth, and with the flood tide the wind was coming up in gusts from the southeast that seemed to bode angry weather. By that time no two Danish ships were in company, and the tide was setting them out to sea.

"Here is a gale coming," said Kolgrim, looking at the sky and the whitening wave crests. "We had best get our ships into this haven while we can."

It seemed that Thord was of the same mind, for now he was heading homeward, and the other Saxons were putting about and following him. So I got men into the best of the ships we had taken, and waited till Thord in Odda's ship led the way, and so followed into Poole Harbour.

Well it was for us that we had refuge so handy. For by noonday the gale was blowing from the southwest, and two Danish ships were wrecked in trying to gain the harbour--preferring to yield to us rather than face the sea, with a lee shore, rocky and hopeless, waiting for them.

We went into the Poole inlet, which is on the eastern side of the wide waters of the haven, and there found good berths enough. The village was empty, save for a few Saxon fishermen, who hailed us joyfully. And then Odda made for us as good a feast as he might in the best house that was there, bidding every shipmaster to it. Merry enough were all, though we had but ship fare; for the Saxons had great hopes from this victory.

Now Odda made much of what I had done--though it was little enough--saying that I and my men deserved well of Alfred, and that he hoped that we should stay with him for this winter, which would perhaps see the end of the war.

"Why," said I, "things would have been much the same if I had not been here."

"That they would not," he answered. "I should have blundered past this place in the night, and so lost the Danes altogether; or if I had not done that, they would soon have found out what state my men were in. You should have heard old Thord rate them into order; it is in my mind that he even called me--Odda the ealdorman--hard names in his broad Norse tongue. But at least he gave us somewhat more to think of than the sickness that comes of heaving planks that will by no means keep steady for a moment."

He laughed heartily at himself, and then added:

"Good King Alfred thought not at all of that matter. Now I can shift the whole credit of this victory to your shoulders, and then he will not believe that I am the born sea captain that he would have me think myself."

"I will not have that," I said, "for I have not deserved it."

"Ay; but, I pray you, let me put it from myself, else shall I be sent to sea again without any one to look to for advice," he said earnestly, and half laughing at the same time. "I did but take command of this fleet because the king could find no one else at a pinch. Heaven defend me from such a charge again!"

"Now you have only the Exeter Danes to deal with," I said.

"How many men might these ships have held?" he asked.

"Maybe five thousand," I answered.

Thereat his face changed, and he rose up from his seat at the high table, and said that he would go down to see that the ships were safe, for the gale was blowing heavily as the night fell.

So we went outside the house, and called a man, telling him to find one of the Poole fishermen and bring him to speak to us.

"There were twelve thousand Danes in Wareham," he said, "for more have come lately. I thought they would all have been in the ships."

"If that had been possible, not one would have seen the morning's light," I answered, "for their ships are lost in this gale certainly."

Now I will say that I was right. The wrecks strewed the shore of Dorset and Hants next morning; and if any men won to land, there waited for them the fishers and churls, who hated them. No Danish fleet was left in the channel after that gale was spent.

When the fisher came, he told us that as many more Danes were left in Wareham, and that those from Poole had fled thither when they saw what had happened to the fleet.

"Shall you march on Wareham and scatter them, or will they fall on us here?" I asked; for we had no more than two thousand men at most.

"I would that I knew what they thought of this business," he answered; "but I shall not move tonight. It is far by land, and I suppose we could not get the ships up in the dark."

So he posted pickets along the road to Wareham, and we went back to the house for a while. And presently, as it grew dark, a wild thought came into my mind. I would go to Wareham with a guide, and see what I could find out of the Danish plans. Maybe there were fewer men than was thought, or they might be panic-stricken at our coming in this wise; or, again, they might march on us, and if so, we should have to get to sea again, to escape from double our numbers.

Now the more I thought of this, the more I grew bent on going, for I was sure that we must know what was going on. And at last I took Odda aside while Harek sang among the men, and told him what I would do.

At first he was against my running the risk; but I told him that a Norseman might go safely where a Saxon could not among the Danes, and at last I persuaded him. Then I called Kolgrim, and we went out together into the moonlight and the wind, to find the fisherman we had spoken with already and get him to act as guide. I think that Odda did not expect to see either of us again; and when I came to know more of Saxons, I learned that he trusted me most fully, for many thanes would have thought it likely that I went on some treacherous errand.

Chapter IV. Jarl Osmund's Daughter.

To my mind, no gale seems so wild as one that comes at the time of full moon, when the clouds break up and fly in great masses of black and silver against the deeper sky beyond, while bright light and deepest shadow chase each other across land and sea beneath them. Kolgrim and I stood under the lee of a shed, waiting for the fisher to get his boat afloat, and looked out on bending trees and whitened water, while beyond the harbour we could see the great downs, clear cut and dark, almost as well as by day, so bright it was.

It was low water now, which was good for us, for the winding channels that lead up to Wareham were sheltered under their bare banks. We could hear the thunder of the surf along the rocky coast outside, when the wind ceased its howling for a moment; and at high water the haven had been well nigh too stormy for a small boat. Now we should do best to go by water, for wind was with us; though, unless the gale dropped very quickly, we could not return in her, for there would be a heavy sea and tide against us if we could get away before it turned, while if we were long wind against tide would be worse yet.

The fisherman was eager to help us against the Danes, who had made him work for nought; and so in half an hour we were flying up the haven on the first rise of tide, and the lights of Wareham town grew plainer every moment. From the number of twinkling sparks that flitted here and there, it would seem that many folk were waking, even if some movement were not on hand.

Presently we turned into the channel that bends to the southwest from the more open water, and the town was before us. The fisher took to his oars now, lowering the scrap of sail that had been enough to drive us very swiftly before the gale so far.

Wareham stands on the tongue of land between two rivers' mouths, and the tide was setting us into the northward of these. That was the river one would have to cross in coming to or from Poole, and maybe we should learn as much there as anywhere.

There were three ships on the mud, but even in the moonlight it was plain that they were not seaworthy. There were wide gaps in their bulwarks, which none had tried to mend, and the stem head of one was gone.

"These ships were hurt in the storm of last week," the fisher said, as we drifted past them; "there was hardly one that came in unhurt. But the Danes were eager to go, and mended them as they could."

Perhaps that was partly the reason why we gained so easy a victory, I thought at the time, and afterwards knew that I was right. They had suffered very much, while we lay across channel in safety.

There loomed before us the timbers of a strong bridge that had been over the north river, when we were fairly in it and under the nearer houses of the town. But now it was broken down, and the gap in its middle was too wide for hasty repair.

"When was this done?" I asked the fisherman.

"Since yesterday," he answered.

Now this seemed to me to indicate that the Danes meant to guard against attack by land from Poole; also that they overrated our numbers, which was probable in any case, seeing that a fleet had fled from before us.

There were wharves on the seaward side of the bridge, but none were beyond; and the houses stood back from the water, so that there was a sort of open green between it and them. There were no people about, but we could hear shouts from the town now and then.

"Let us go ashore and speak with some one," I said; "it is of no use our biding here on the water."

Kolgrim and I were fully armed, and had boat cloaks with us which covered us well, and we thought none would question who we were if we mixed among the men in some inn or other gathering place. So we bade the fisher wait for us, and found the stairs, and went to the wide green along the waterside, and across it to the houses, which were mostly poor enough here.

Many of them stood open, and in one a fire burned on the hearth, but all were empty. So we turned into a street that led seemingly from one bridge to the other across the town. Here men were going hither and thither with torches, and groups were outside some of the houses. To the nearest of these I went, as if I had all right to be in the place.

They were bringing goods out of the house, and loading a cart with them.

"Here is a flitting," said Kolgrim, "and another or two are on hand yonder."

I stayed a man who came past me from out of a house.

"I have fled from Poole," I said. "What is in the wind here? Are we to leave Wareham also?"

"If you come from Poole, you should know that it is time we did so," he answered shortly. "I suppose you saw the whole business."

"So I did," I answered. "What are the orders?"

"Pack up and quit with all haste," said he. "You had better get to work if you have aught to save."

"Shall we go to Exeter, or back to Mercia?" I said.

"Exeter they say; but I know not. Why not go and ask Jarl Osmund himself--or follow the crowd and hinder no one with questions?"

He hurried on; but then some men began to question us about the doings off Swanage, and Kolgrim told them such tales that they shivered, and soon we had a crowd round us listening. Nor did I like to hurry away, for I heard a man say that we were Northmen, by our voices. But there were plenty of our folk among the Danes.

Then came a patrol of horsemen down the street, and they bade the loiterers hurry. I drew Kolgrim into an open doorway, and stood there till they passed, hearing them rate their fellows for delay.

"Wareham will be empty tomorrow," I said. "Now we can go; we have learned enough."

Still I would see more, for there seemed no danger. Every man was thinking of himself. So we went across the town, and as we came near the western bridge the crowd grew very thick.

We heard before long that the army was as great as Odda had thought, and that they were going to Exeter. Already the advance guard had gone forward, but this train of followers would hardly get clear of the town before daylight. They had heard great accounts of our numbers, and I wished we had brought the ships up here at once. There would have been a rout of the Danes.

But the place was strange to me, and to Odda also, so that we could not be blamed.

We got back by the way we came, and then knew that we could in no way take the boat to Poole. The gale was raging at its highest, and thatch was flying from the exposed roofs. It would be dead against us; and the sea was white with foam, even in the haven. So we must go by road, and that was a long way. But we must get back to Odda, for he should be in Wareham before the Danes learned, maybe, that their flight was too hurried.

Now it seemed to me that to leave Wareham was not so safe as to come into it, for no Dane would be going away from the place. However, the bridge was down; and if it had not been done in too great haste, any fugitives from the country would have come in. So that maybe we should meet no one on the road that goes along the shore of the great haven.

The fisherman ferried us over to the opposite shore, and then tied his boat to the staging of the landing place, saying that he was well known and in no danger. He would sleep now, and bring his boat back when the wind fell. So we left him, thanking him for his goodwill.

Grumbling, as men will, we set out on our long walk in the gale. We could not miss the road, for it never left the curves of the shore, and all we had to do was to be heedful of any meetings. There might be outposts even yet, watching against surprise.

However, we saw no man in the first mile, and then were feeling more secure, when we came to a large farmstead which stood a short bowshot back from the road, with a lane of its own leading to the great door. What buildings there were seemed to be behind it, and no man was about; but there was light shining from one of the high windows, as if some one were inside, and plain to be seen in the moonlight were two horses tied by the stone mounting block at the doorway.

"Here is a chance for us, master," said my comrade, coming to a stand in the roadway. "I must try to steal these horses for ourselves. If Danes are in the place, they have doubtless stolen them; and if Saxons, they will get them back."

"There will be no Saxon dwelling so near the Danes," I said. "Maybe the place is full of Danes--some outpost that is careless."

"Careless enough," said Kolgrim. "If they are careless for three minutes more, they have lost their horses."

Then we loosened our swords in their sheaths, and drew our seaxes, and went swiftly up the grassy lane. The wind howled round the house so that none would hear the clank of mail, which we could not altogether prevent. But the horses heard us, and one shifted about and whinnied as if glad to welcome us.

At that we ran and each took the bridle of that next him, and cut the halter that was tied to the rings in the wall, looking to see the doors thrown open at any moment. Then we leaped to the saddles and turned to go. The hoofs made a great noise on the paving stones before the doorway, yet there was no sound from inside the house.

That seemed strange to me, and I sat still, looking back with the horse's head turned towards the main road.

"Stay not, master," Kolgrim said. "'Tis some outpost, and the men have slept over the farmhouse ale. Maybe the stables behind are full of horses. Have a care, master; the door opens!"

He was going; but I waited for a moment, half expecting to see a spear point come first, and my hand was on my sword hilt. But the great heavy door swung slowly, as if the one who opened it had trouble with its weight. So I must needs see who came. Maybe it was some old man or woman whose terror I could quiet in a few words.

Then the red firelight from within shone out on me, and in the doorway, with arms raised to post and door on either hand, stood a tall maiden, white robed, with gold on neck and arm. The moonlight on her seemed weird with the glow of the fire shining through the edges of her hood and sleeves. I could see her face plainly, and it was fair and troubled, but there was no fear in her looks.

"Father, is this you?" she said quietly.

I could make no answer to that, and she looked intently at me; for the moon was beyond me, and both Kolgrim and I would seem black against it, as she came from the light within, while the wind, keen with salt spray, was blowing in her face.

"Who is it?" she said again. "I can scarcely see for moon and wind in my eyes."

"Friends, lady," I said, for that at least was true in a way.

"Where are my horses? Have you seen aught of our thralls, who should have left them?" she asked, looking to whence we had just taken the beasts.

Now I was ashamed to have taken them, for she was so plainly alone and helpless, and I could not understand altogether how it could be so. I was sure that she was Danish, too.

"How is it that you have not fled, lady?" I asked. "Surely you should have gone."

"Ay; but the thralls fled when they heard the news. Has not my father sent you back for me?"

This seemed a terrible plight for the maiden, and I knew not what to say or do. She could not be left in the way of our Saxons if they came on the morrow, and I could not take her to Poole. And so, lest I should terrify her altogether, I made up my mind even as she looked to me for an answer.

"I think your father is kept in Wareham in some way. Does he look for you there?"

"Ay, surely," she answered; but there was a note as of some new fear in her voice. "Has aught befallen him? Have the Saxons come?"

"All is well in Wareham yet," I answered. "Now we will take you to your father. But we are strangers, as you may see."

Then I called to Kolgrim, who was listening open eyed to all this, and backed away from the door a little.

"What is this madness, master?" he whispered hoarsely.

"No madness at all. Ten minutes' ride to Wareham with the maiden, give her to the fisherman to take to her friends, and then ride away--that is all. Then we shall be in Poole long before any look for us, for we are in luck's way."

Kolgrim laughed.

"Strange dangers must I run with you, master; but that is what one might look for with Ranald of the Sword."

Then I got off the horse, which was very strong and seemed quiet, and went to the maiden again.

"It will be best for you to come with us, lady," I said "we will see you safely to Wareham."

The light fell on my arms now, and they were splendid enough, being Harald Fairhair's gift, which I had put on for the fight, seeing that the men loved to see their king go bravely, and being, moreover, nowise loth to do so myself. She seemed to take heart--for she was well nigh weeping now--when she saw that I was not some wandering soldier of the great host.

"My horses, two of them should be here," she said. "I bade the thralls leave them when they fled."

So she thought not that we had loosed them, and did not know her own in the moonlight. Maybe she had no knowledge as to which of many had been left, and I was glad of that, for so her fear was less.

"You must ride with us," I said, "and I would ask you to come quickly; even now the host is leaving Wareham."

"Ay, is that so? Then my father is busy," she said, and then she faltered a little, and looked at me questioningly. "I cannot go without my nurse, and she is very sick. I think she sleeps now. Men feared her sickness so that we brought her here from the town. But indeed there is nought to fear; there is no fever or aught that another might take from her."

Then I grew fairly anxious, for this was more than I had looked for. I knew that it was likely that she would soon be missed and sought for; yet I could not think of leaving her to that chance, with the bridge broken moreover.

I gave the bridle to Kolgrim then to hold.

"Let me see your nurse," I said gently; "I have some skill in these troubles."

She led me into the house without a word. All the lower story was in one great room, with a hearth and bright fire thereon in the centre. Beyond that was a low bed, to which the maiden went. A very old woman, happed in furs and heavy blankets, lay on it, and it needed but one look to tell me that she needed no care but the last. Past need of flight was she, for she was dead, though so peacefully that her watcher had not known it.

"The sleep is good, is it not?" the maiden said, looking anxiously into my face.

"It is good, lady," I answered, taking off my helm. "It is the best sleep of all--the sleep that heals all things."

The maiden looked once at the quiet face, and once more at me, with wide eyes, and then she knew what I meant, and turned quickly from me and wept silently.

I stood beside her, not daring to speak, and yet longing to be on the road. And so still were we that Kolgrim got off his horse and came to the door and called me, though not loudly.

I stepped back to him.

"Come again in a few minutes and say one word--'Saxons'" I whispered, "then we shall go."

He nodded and drew back. I think the maiden had not heard me move, for she was bent over the bed and what lay thereon. It seemed very long to me before I heard my comrade at the door.

"Saxons, master!" he said loudly.

"Say you so?" I answered, and then I touched the maiden's arm gently.

"Lady, we must go quickly," I said. "The dame is past all help of ours, and none can harm her. Come, I pray you."

She stood up then, still looking away from me, and I drew the covering over the still face she gazed at.

"You must leave her, and I know these Saxons will not wrong the dead," said I gently. "Your father will miss you."

"I am keeping you also in danger," she answered bravely. "I will come."

"Loth to go am I," she said, as she gathered her wrappings to her and made ready very quickly, "for it seems hard. But hard things come to many in time of war."

After that she ceased weeping, and was, as I thought, very brave in this trouble, which was indeed great to her. And when she was clad in outdoor gear, she bent once more over the bed as in farewell, while I turned away to Kolgrim and made ready the horses. Then she came, and mounted behind me on a skin that I had taken from a chair before the hearth.

Then we were away, and I was very glad. The good horse made nothing of the burden, and we went quickly. Many a time had I ridden double, with the rough grip of some mail-shirted warrior round my waist, as we hurried back to the ships after a foray; but this was the first time I had had charge of a lady, and it was in a strange time and way enough. I do not know if it was in the hurry of flight, or because they had none, but the horses had no saddles such as were for ladies' use.

So I did not speak till we were half a mile from the house, and then came a hill, and we walked, because I feared to discomfort my companion. Then I said:

"Lady, we are strangers, and know not to whom we speak nor to whom we must take you."

There was a touch of surprise in her voice as she answered:

"I am the Lady Thora, Jarl Osmund's daughter."

Then I understood how this was the chief to whom the man I spoke with first had bidden me go for orders. It was plain now that he was up and down among the host ordering all things, and deeming his daughter in safety all the while. He had not had time to learn how his cowardly folk had fled and left their mistress, fearing perhaps the sickness of the old dame as much as the Saxon levies.

Now no more was said till we came to the riverside, where the flood tide was roaring through the broken timbers of the bridge. The fisher slept soundly despite the noise of wind and water, and Kolgrim had some trouble in waking him.

"How goes the flight?" I asked him when he came ashore with the boat's painter in his hand.

"Faith, master, I know not. I have slept well," he said.

Now by this time it seemed to me that I ought to take the lady into a safe place, and I would go myself rather than leave her to the fisherman, who was rough, and hated the Danes heartily, as I knew. Moreover, I had a new plan in my head which pleased me mightily. Then I thought that if I were to meet any man who suspected me, which was not likely, the Lady Thora would be pass enough for me. So I told Kolgrim to bide here for me, and he said at first that he must be with me. However, I made him stay against his will at last, telling him what I thought.

Then the fisher put us across quickly, and went back to the far side to wait my return.

I asked Thora where I must take her to find the jarl.

"To his house, surely," she said.

"I do not know the way from here," I answered; "I fear you must lead me."

"As you will," she said, wondering. "It is across the town certainly."

That was bad for me, perhaps, but I should find that out presently. So we went across the open, and came to the road through the town along which I had been before. It was clearer, though there were yet many people about.

Now when we were in the shadow of the first houses, Thora stopped suddenly and looked hard at me.

"Will you tell me if I am heading you into danger?" she said.

"What danger is possible?" I answered. "There are no Saxons here yet."

"Not one?" she said meaningly. "I may be wrong--it does seem unlikely but I think you do not belong to us. Your speech is not like ours altogether, and your helm is gold encircled, as if you were a king."

"Lady," I said, "why should you think that I am not of your people? Let us go on to the jarl."

"Now I know that you are not. Oh, how shall I thank you for this?"

Then she glanced at my helm again, and drew a sudden little quick breath.

"Is it possible that you are Alfred of Wessex? It were like what they say of him to do as you have done for a friendless maiden."

Then she caught my hand and held it in both of hers, looking half fearfully at me.

"Lady," I said, "I am not King Alfred, nor would I be. Come, let us hasten."

"I will take you no further," she said then. "Now I am sure that you are of the Northmen that were seen with the Saxons. You are not of us, and I shall lose you your life."

Then came the quick trot of horses, and I saw a little troop coming down the street, their arms flashing in the streaks of moonlight between the houses.

"I will see you in good hands, Lady Thora," I answered. "Who are these coming?"

"It is my father," she said, and drew me back deeper into shadow.

After the horsemen and beside them ran men who bore planks and ropes, and it was plain that the jarl had found out his loss, and hastened to bridge the gap and cross the river.

I saw that I could keep up the pretence no longer.

"Let me walk behind you as your servant," I said. "If any heed me, I pray you make what tale you can for me."

"What can I say to you in thanks?" she cried quickly, and letting go my hand which she yet held. "If you are slain, it is my fault. Tell me your name at least."

"Ranald Vemundsson, a Northman of King Alfred's," I said. "Now I am your servant--ever."

Then Thora left my side suddenly, and ran forward to meet the foremost horseman--for they were close to us--calling aloud to Osmund to stay. And he reined up and leaped from his horse with a cry of joy, and took her in his arms for a moment.

I got my cloak around me, pulling the hood over my helm, and stood in the shadow where I was. I saw the jarl lift his daughter into the saddle, and the whole troop turned to go back. The footmen cast down their burdens where each happened to be, and went quickly after them; and I was turning to go my way also, when a man came riding back towards me.

"Ho, comrade," he said, "hasten after us. Mind not the things left in the boat. There is supper ere we go."

I lifted my hand, and he turned his horse and rode away, paying no more heed to me. That was a good tale of things left that Thora had made in case I was seen to be going back to the boat.

Then I waxed light hearted enough, and thought of my other plan. Kolgrim saw me coming, and the boat was ready.

"Have you flint and steel?" I said to the fisher as I got into the boat.

"Ay, master, and tinder moreover, dry in my cap."

"Well, then, take me to those ships we saw. I have a mind to scare these Danes."

It was a heavy pull against the sea to where they lay afloat now, though it was not far. I fired all three in the cabins under the fore deck, so that, as their bows were towards the town, the light would not be seen till I was away.

Then we went swiftly back to Kolgrim, and as I mounted and rode off, the blaze flared up behind us, for the tarred timbers burned fiercely in the wind.

"That will tell Odda that the Danes are flying. And maybe it will save Wareham town from fire, for they will think we are on them. So I have spoiled Jarl Osmund's supper for him."

Then I minded that this would terrify the Lady Thora maybe, and that put me out of conceit with my doings for a moment. But it was plain that she was brave enough, for there were many things to fray her in the whole of this matter, though perhaps it was because Kolgrim stayed beyond the river that she made so sure that I was a man of King Alfred's and no friend to the Danes.

So we rode away, pleased enough with the night's work, and reached Poole in broad daylight, while the gale was slackening. Well pleased was Odda to see me back, and to hear my news.

Then he asked me what I would do next. There seemed to be no more work at sea, and yet he would have me speak with King Alfred and take some reward from him. And I told him that the season grew late, and that I would as soon stay in England for this winter as anywhere.

"What will you do next in the matter of these Danes, however?" was my question.

Then he said:

"I must chase them through the country till they are within the king's reach. He has the rest pent in Exeter, and there will be trouble if they sail out to join these. I must follow them, therefore, end send men to Alfred to warn him. Then he will know what to do. Now I would ask you to take the ships back into the river Exe and join us there."

I would do that willingly, and thought that if the wind held fair after the gale ended, I might be there before he joined the king by land. But I should have to wait for a shift to the eastward before sailing.

So Odda brought his men ashore, and marched on Wareham and thence after the Danes, not meaning to fight unless some advantage showed itself, for they were too many, but to keep them from harming the country. And I waited for wind to take me westward.

Then the strange Norsemen left us. They had gained much booty in the Danish ships, for they carried what had been won from the Saxons, and what plunder should be taken was to be their share in due for their services. They were little loss, for they were masterless vikings who might have given trouble at any time if no plunder was to be had, and I was not sorry to see them sail away to join Rolf Ganger in France.

Now these men would have followed me readily, and so I should have been very powerful at sea, or on any shore where I cared to land. But Odda had made me feel so much that I was one in his counsel, and a friend whom he valued and trusted, that I had made this warfare against the Danes my own quarrel, as it were in his company. Already I had a great liking for him, and the more I heard of Alfred the king, the more I wished to see him. At the least, a man who could build ships like these, having every good point of the best I knew, and better than any ever heard of before, was worth speaking with. I thought I knew somewhat of the shipwright's craft, and one thinks much of the wisdom of the man who is easily one's master in anything wherein one has pride.

Moreover, Alfred's men were wont to speak of him with little fear, but as if longing for his praise. And I thought that wonderful, knowing only Harald Fairhair and the dread of him.

Chapter V. Two Meetings in England.

It was not long before the shift of wind that I looked for came, and at once I took all the ships round to the river Exe. Odda had left me all the seamen he had, and they were enough for the short, fair passage. We came to the haven in the river, and there heard what news there was, and it was good enough. Odda had sent well-mounted men to reach the king by roads away from the retreating Danes, and he had been ready for them. He drew off his levies from before the walls of the town, and let his enemies pass him; then he and Odda fell on their rear and drove them into Exeter, and there was holding them. It was well done; for though the host sallied from the town to meet the newcomers, they gained nothing but a share in the rout that followed when Odda closed on the rear guard and the king charged the flank.

Now we heard that as soon as we landed. And then I had my first knowledge of the ways of a Saxon levy. For no sooner were the ships berthed than their crews began to leave them, making for their homes.

One or two men I caught in the act of leaving in the early morning, and spoke sharply to them, for it seemed that soon there would be ships enough and not a man to tend them. Whereon they answered:

"We have done what we were called up for, and more also. Now may others take our places. What more would you have? We have won our victory, and the ships are not needed for a while."

So they went, and nothing I could say would stay them. I waxed angry on that, and I thought I might as well sail for Ireland as not. There seemed no chance of doing aught here, where men would throw away what they had won of advantage.

So I went back to my own ship and sat under the after awning, in no good temper. Thord and Kolgrim were yet busy in and about the vessels, making all secure, and setting men to work on what needed repairing. Presently Harek the scald came and sat with me, and I grumbled to my heart's content about this Saxon carelessness and throwing away of good luck.

Many Saxons--men from camp, and freemen of the place, and some thanes--came, as one might expect, to stare at the ships and their prizes. I paid no heed to them as the day went on, only wishing that Odda would come and speak to me about his doings, for I had sent word to him that we were in the river. Sometimes a thane would stay and speak with me from the wharf alongside which my own ship was with one or two others, and they were pleasant enough, though they troubled me with over many thanks, which was Odda's fault. However, I will say this, that if every man made as little of his own doings and as much of those of his friends as did the honest ealdorman, it were well in some ways.

By and by, while we were talking, having got through my grumble, Kolgrim came along the shore with some Saxon noble whom he had met; and this stranger was asking questions about each ship that he passed. I suppose that Kolgrim had answered many such curious folk already; for when he came near and we could hear what he was saying, I was fain to laugh, for, as sailors will, he was telling the landsman strange things.

"What do we pull up the anchor with?" he was saying. "Why, with yonder big rope that goes from masthead to bows." and he pointed to the great mainstay of our ship. "One must have a long purchase, if you know what that is."

"Ah, 'tis wonderful," said the Saxon.

Then he caught my eye, and saw that I was smiling. He paid no heed to me, however, but looked long at the ship that lay astern of ours--one of the captured Danes. Thord had set a gang of shore folk to bend the sail afresh to a new yard, for the old one had been strained in the gale that came before the fight.

"What are those men doing, friend?" he asked Kolgrim directly.

"Bending a sail," answered my comrade listlessly, trusting, as it would seem, to the sea language for puzzlement enough to the landsman.

"So," said the Saxon, quite quietly. "It was in my mind that when a sail was bent to the yard it was bent with the luff to the fore end thereof."

At which words Kolgrim started, in a way, and looked first at the riggers and then back at the Saxon, who moved no muscle of his face, though one might see that his eyes twinkled. And I looked at the riggers also, and saw that the Saxon was right, and that the men had the square-cut sail turned over with the leech forward and the luff aft. The sail was half laced to the yard, and none but a man who knew much of ships would have seen that aught was wrong.

Then Kolgrim's face was so red, and angry, and full of shame all at once, that I had the best laugh at him that had come to me for many a day. And he did not bide with the Saxon any longer, but went on board the ship hastily, and said what he had to say to the riggers. The Saxon stood, and looked after him with a smile breaking over his pleasant face, and I thought that maybe I owed him some amends for my comrade's rough jesting, though indeed he had his revenge.

So I came ashore and spoke to him. He was a slight, brown-haired man of about thirty, bearded and long-haired after the Saxon fashion, and I thought he seemed to be recovering from some wound or sickness that had made him white and thin. He wore his beard long and forked, which may have made him look thinner; but he seemed active and wiry in his movements--one of those men who make up for want of strength by quickness and mastery of their weapons. Soberly dressed enough he was, but the cloth of his short cloak and jerkin was very rich, and he had a gold bracelet and brooch that seemed to mark him as high in rank.

"My comrade has been well caught, thane," I said; "he will be more careful what tales he tells the next comer. But I think he was tired of giving the same answers to the same questions to all who come to see us."

"Likely enough," the Saxon answered, laughing a little. "I asked to see the prizes and the vikings' ships, and he showed me more than I expected."

Then he looked along the line of vessels that he had not yet passed, and added:

"I thought there were more Norse ships with Odda."

I told him how the other vikings had left us with their plunder at Wareham, saying that I thought they could well be spared at that time.

"However," I said, "I did not count on the Saxons leaving their vessels so soon."

"Then I take it that I am speaking with King Ranald, of whom Odda has so much to say," he said, without answering my last words.

"I am Ranald Vemundsson," I said; "but this ship is all my kingdom now. Harald Fairhair has the land that should have been mine. I am but a sea king."

Then he held out his hand, saying that there was much for which every Saxon should thank me, and I passed that by as well as I could, though I was pleased with the hearty grip he gave me.

"So long as Odda is satisfied it is enough," I said. "If I have helped him a little, I have helped a man who is worth it."

"Well," said the thane, "you seem to be pleased with one another. Now I should like to see this ship of yours, of which he has so much to say."

We went over her, and it was plain that this thane knew what he was talking about. I wondered that the king had not set him in command instead of Odda, who frankly said what was true--that he was no sailor. I supposed that this man, however, was not of high rank enough to lead so great a gathering of Saxons, and so I said nothing to him about it.

By and by we sat on the after deck with Harek, and I had ale brought to us, and we talked of ship craft of all sorts. Presently, however, he said:

"What shall you do now--if one may ask?"

"I know not. When I sailed from Wareham, I thought to have seen more sea service with Alfred your king. But now his men are going home, and in a day or two, at this rate, there will be none left to man the ships."

"We can call them up again when need is," he answered.

"They should not go home till the king sends them," I said. "This is not the way in which Harald Fairhair made himself master of Norway. Once his men are called out they know that they must bide with him till he gives them rest and sends them home with rewards. It is his saying that one sets not down the hammer till the nail is driven home, and clinched moreover."

"That is where the Danes are our masters," the Saxon said, very gravely. "Our levies fight and disperse. It was not so in the time of the great battles round Reading that brought us peace, for they never had time to do so. Then we won. Now the harvest wants gathering. Our people know they are needed at home and in the fields."

"They must learn to know that home and fields will be better served by their biding in arms while there is a foe left in the land. What says Alfred the king?" I said.

"Alfred sees this as well as you, or as any one but our freemen," he answered; "but not yet can he make things go as he knows they should. This is the end at which he ever aims, and I think he will teach his people how to fight in time. I know this, that we shall have no peace until he does."

"Your king can build a grand ship, but she is of no use without men in her day by day, till they know every plank of her."

"Ay," said the Saxon; "but that will come in time. It is hard to know how to manage all things."

"Why," I said, "if the care of a ship is a man's business, for that he will care. You cannot expect him to care for farm and ship at once, when the farm is his living, and the ship but a thing that calls him away from it."

"What then?"

"Pay the shipman to mind the sea, that is all. Make his ship his living, and the thing is done."

"It seems to me," the thane said, "that this can be done. I shall tell the king your words."

"As you will," I answered; "they are plain enough. I would say also that Harald our king has about him paid warriors whose living is to serve him, and more who hold lands on condition that they bear arms for him at any time."

Now Harek had listened to all this, and could tell the thane more of Harald's ordering of things than I; so he took up the talk for a time, and presently asked about the war and its beginning.

"Faith," answered the Saxon, with a grim smile, "I cannot tell when the war began, for that was when the first Danes came to the English shores. But if you mean the trouble that is on hand now, it is easily told. Ten years has this host been in England--coming first with Ingvar and Halfden and Hubba, the three sons of Lodbrok. Ingvar has gone away, and Guthrum takes his place. Halfden is in Northumbria, Hubba is in Wales, and Guthrum is king over East Anglia and overlord of Mercia. It is Guthrum against whom we are fighting."

"He is minded to be overlord of all England," said Harek.

"That is to be seen if a Dane shall be so," the Saxon answered, flushing. "We beat them at first, as I have said, and have had peace till last year. Then they came to Wareham from East Anglia. There they were forced to make peace, and they swore on the holy ring [vi] to depart from Wessex; and we, on our part, swore peace on the relics of the holy saints. Whereon, before the king, Alfred, was ware of their treachery, they fell on our camp, slew all our horsemen, and marched here. Then we gathered the levies again--ay, I know why you look so impatiently, King Ranald--and came here after them. As for the rest, you have taken your part. Now we have them all inside these walls, and I think we have done."

Then his face grew dark, and he added:

"But I cannot tell. What can one do with oath breakers of this sort?"

Then I said:

"Surely you do not look for the men of one chief to be bound by what another promises?"

He looked wonderingly at me for a moment, and then said:

"How should it be that the oath of their king should not bind the people?"

"Why," said I, "you have spoken of several chiefs. If Guthrum chooses to make peace, that is not Halfden's business, or Hubba's, or that of any chief who likes it not. One is as free as the other."

"What mean you? I say that Guthrum and his chiefs swore by the greatest oath they knew to return to Mercia."

"If they swore by the holy ring, there is no doubt that they who swore would keep the oath. But that does not bind those who were against the peace making. So I suppose that they who held not with the peace made by the rest fell on you, when your levies went home after their wont. One might have known they would do so."

Thereat the thane was silent for a while, and I saw that he was troubled. It seemed to be a new thought to him at this time that the Danish hosts in England were many, and each free to act in the way its own chief thought best, uniting now and then, and again separating. This he must needs have learned sooner or later, but the knowledge came first to him there before Exeter walls.

Presently he said:

"I have believed that all the Danes were as much one under Guthrum their king as are my folk under theirs. I cannot see the end of this war."

"It will end when Alfred the king is strong enough always to have men in the field to face every leader that will fall on him," Harek said. "What King Ranald says is true. It is as if his own father had minded what Harald had sworn in the old days."

"Wherefore Harald brought all Norway under him, that every man should mind what he said," the Saxon answered.

Then came three or four more thanes along the shore, and he rose up and waved his hand to them.

"Here are more butts for Kolgrim," he said, laughing. "Now, King Ranald, I must go to my friends. But I have learned much. I think you must speak with the king before you go, and I will tell him all you have said."

"Maybe we shall meet again," said I, taking his offered hand. "I think I would see Alfred; but he is over wise, from all accounts, to learn aught from me."

"King Alfred says that wisdom comes little by little, and by learning from every one. I belong to the court, and so shall surely meet you if you do come to speak to him."

Then I asked the thane's name.

"Godred [vii] men say it is," he answered, laughing; "but that means better counsel than belongs to me."

So he went ashore and joined the thanes, who had gone slowly along the road, and we lost sight of him.

"Yonder goes a pleasant comrade enough," I said to Harek.

"Ay," the scald answered; "but if that is not Alfred the king himself, I am much in error."

"It is not likely. I think he is a bigger man and older, from all accounts," I said carelessly. "Moreover, he would not have put up with Kolgrim's jests as he did."

"One knows not; but I thought he spoke of 'my folk' once. And he seemed to ask more than would a simple thane, and in a different way."

However, it seemed to me that Harek had found a marvel for himself, and I laughed at him for supposing that Alfred the king would come there to speak to any man.

Now towards evening Odda came, and with him many servants and a train of wagons. He would make a feast for us in the best house of the village, by the king's order. Every one of us was called, and all the leading Saxon shipmen, when all was ready, and it was a kingly feast enough.

While they were making it ready, the ealdorman came to me on board the ship, and welcomed me in most friendly wise.

"I have a message for you, King Ranald," he said presently. "Some thanes have been to me from the king, and he bids me ask you to come and speak with him."

"I saw a thane here this morning who was anxious for me to see the king," I said. "A pleasant man enough--one Godred."

"Ay, Godred is pleasant enough," Odda said, smiling, "but he is a terrible man for asking questions."

He laughed again, as if he knew the man well, and was pleased to think of him and his ways.

"None of his questions are foolish, however," I said. "I was pleased with him."

"It is well if you pleased him, for he is a powerful man at court," said Odda.

"I do not know if I pleased him, or if it makes any difference to me what power he has," I said carelessly. "If I want any man to speak for me to the king--which is not likely--I should come to you first."

"Speak for yourself," laughed Odda, "that is the best way with Alfred."

So we planned to go to Exeter with the next morning's light. Odda would bide here for the night, after the feast.

Now after we had finished eating, and the ale and mead and the wine the king had sent in our honour were going round, and the gleemen were singing at times, there came a messenger into the house, and brought me a written message from the king himself, as he said.

"Much good are these scratches to me," said I to Odda. "Can you read them?"

"I can read nought but what is written in a man's face," he said.

So I gave the scroll to Harek, who sat next me, thinking that maybe the scald could read it. He pored over it for a while.

"It is of no use, king," he said. "It is in my mind that I know which is the right way up of the writing, but I am not sure."

So I laughed, and asked aloud if any man present could read. There were a good many thanes and franklins present to feast in our honour.

Then rose up a man, in a long brown hooded habit girt with a cord, from below the salt where he sat among the servants. He had a long beard, but was very bald. His hair grew in a thick ring round his head; which was strange, for he seemed young.

"I am here, ealdorman," he said to Odda; "I will read for King Ranald."

Now all eyes turned to see who spoke, and in a moment Odda rose up hastily and went down the long room till he came to where the man stood. Then I was amazed, for the ealdorman went on one knee before him, and said:

"Good my lord, I knew not that you were here among the crowd. I pray you come to the high seat."

"When will you remember that titles and high places are no longer pleasing to me?" the man said wearily. "I tire of them all. Rise up, Odda, my friend, and let me be."

"I will not rise without your blessing, nevertheless," said the ealdorman.

Whereon the man spoke a few words to him softly and quickly, signing with his hand crosswise over him.

Then I said to those about me, who were watching all this in silence:

"Who is this strange man?"

"It is Neot the holy, King Alfred's cousin," one answered, whispering.

"That is a strange dress for an atheling," I said; but they hushed me.

Now it seemed that Odda tried again to draw this Neot to the high table, but he would not come.

Then I said to old Thord, who sat over against me beyond Odda's empty chair:

"This is foolishness; or will he not honour the king's guests?"

But a thane shook his head at me, whispering behind his hand:

"It is humbleness. He has put his rank from him, and will not be held as being above any man."

Then spoke old Thord:

"Maybe he can put his rank away among men who know him not, and that is a good humbleness in a way. But where all know what his birth is, he has but to be humble and kind in ways and speech, and then men will think more thereof than they will if they see him pretending to be a churl."

Now Thord's voice was rough with long years of speaking against the wash of the waves, and the thunder of wind in sail and rigging, and the roll and creak of oars; and as he said this, every one turned towards him, for a silence had fallen on the crowd of folk who watched Neot the king's cousin and his strife with Odda.

So Neot heard, and his face flushed a little, and he looked hard at Thord and smiled curiously, saying:

"In good truth the old warrior is right, and I am foolish to hide here now I am known. Let me go and sit by him."

Then Odda led him to the upper end of the room, and every one rose as he passed by. I drew myself nearer to the ealdorman's place, and made room for him where only the table was between him and Thord, for that bench was full.

So he put his hand on my shoulder and sat down, looking over to Thord, and saying with a quiet smile:

"Thanks for that word in season, friend."

But the old warrior was somewhat ashamed, and did but shift in his seat uneasily.

"Ay, ay," he growled; "I cannot keep my voice quiet."

Neot laughed, and then turned to me and held out his hand for the king's letter, which I gave him.

He ran his eyes over the writing very quickly, and then said:

"Here is nothing private; shall I read aloud?"

But the thanes fell to talking quickly, and I nodded.

"Alfred the king to his cousin Ranald Vemundsson, greeting. Odda the ealdorman of Devon, and one Godred, have spoken to me of yourself--one telling of help given freely and without question of reward or bargain made, and the other of certain plain words spoken this morning. Now I would fain see you, and since the said Godred seems to doubt if you will come to me, I ask it under my own hand thus. For I have thanks to give both to you and your men, and also would ask you somewhat which it is my hope that you will not refuse me. Therefore, my cousin, I would ask you to come with our ealdorman tomorrow and hear all I would say."

Then Neot said,

"That is all. I think you will not refuse so kindly an invitation. The writing is the king's own, and here is his name at the end."

So he showed it me. The letter was better written than the name, as it seemed to me.

"I will take your word for it," I said, laughing as I looked; "but it is a kindly letter, and I will surely come."

"Ay; he has written to you as to an equal," Odda said.

"That is so. Now I would have the good king know that I am not that; I am but a sea king. Maybe he thinks that I shall be a good ally, and makes more of my power than should be. I told Godred the thane as plainly as I could what I was, this morning."

"Why, then," said Neot, smiling, "Godred has told the king, no doubt."

"I hope he has," I answered, "but I doubt it. Nevertheless it is easy to tell the king myself when I see him."

After that we talked about other matters, and it became plain that this Neot was a wonderfully wise man, and, as I thought, a holy one in truth, as they called him. There is that about such an one that cannot be mistaken.

Harek sang for us, and pleased all, and into his song came, as one might suppose, a good deal about the Asir. And then Neot began to ask me a good deal about the old gods, as he called them. I told him what I knew, which was little enough maybe, and so said that Harek knew all about them, and that he should rather ask him.

He did not care to do that, but asked me plainly if I were a Christian.

"How should I be?" I said. "Odda is the first Christian man I have spoken with, to my knowledge. So, if I were likely to leave my own faith, I have not so much as heard of another."

"So you are no hater of Christians?" he said.

"Surely not. Why should I be? I never thought of the matter."

Then he said:

"Herein you Norsemen are not like the Danes, who hate our faith, and slay our priests because of their hatred."

"More likely because Christian means Saxon to them, or else because you have slain them as heathens. Northmen do not trouble about another nation's faith so long as their own is not interfered with. Why should they? Each country has its own ways in this as in other matters."

Thereat Neot was silent, and asked me no more. Hereafter I learned that hatred of race had made the hatred of religion bitter, until the last seemed to be the greatest hatred of all, adding terror and bitterest cruelty to the struggle for mastery.

Presently, before it was very late, Neot rose up and spoke to Odda, bidding him farewell. Then he came to me, and said:

"Tell the king that we have spoken together, and give him this message if you will that I go to my place in Cornwall, and shall be there for a while."

Then he passed to Thord, and took his hard hand and said:

"Good are words that come from an honest heart. I have learned a lesson tonight where I thought to have learned none."

"I marvel that you needed to learn that," Thord said gruffly.

"So do I, friend," answered Neot; "but one is apt to go too far in a matter which one has at heart, sometimes before one is aware. Then is a word in season welcome."

Then he thanked Harek for his songs, and went, the Saxons bowing as he passed down the long table with Odda.

"That is a wise man and a holy," said Thord.

"Ay, truly," answered the thane who had told me about him. "I mind when he and Alfred the king were the haughtiest and most overbearing of princes. But when Neot found out that his pride and wrath and strength were getting the mastery in his heart, he thrust himself down there to overcome them. So he grows more saintlike every day, and has wrought a wondrous change in the king himself. He is the only man to whom Alfred will listen in reproof."

"That is likely," I said, not knowing aught of the holy bishops who were the king's counsellors; "kings brook little of that sort. But why does he wear yon strange dress?"

"He has taken vows on him, and is a hermit," the thane said; but I did not know what he meant at the time.

It was some Saxon way, I supposed, and cared not to ask more.

So it came to pass that I met one of the two most wonderful men in England, and I was to see the other on the morrow. Yet I had no thought that I should care to stay in the land, for it seemed certain from what Odda told me that peace would be made, and peace was not my business nor that of my men.

So in a way I was sorry that the war was at an end, seeing that we came for fighting and should have none.

Then came a thought to me that made me laugh at myself. I was glad, after all, that we were not going sword foremost into Exeter town, because of the Lady Thora, who was there. I suppose it would not have been reasonable had I not had that much thought for the brave maiden whom I had helped out of danger once.

Chapter VI. Alfred the King.

Odda the ealdorman and I rode gaily into the king's camp in the bright August morning, with Harek and Kolgrim and Thord beside us, and after us fifty of my men in their best array; which was saying much, for Einar the jarl was generous, and we had spoiled Halfdan, the king's son, moreover. So there was a shouting when we came to the camp, and men ran together to stare at the vikings and their king.

In the midst of the camp, which was strong enough, and looked out on the old city, flew a banner whereon was a golden dragon--the banner of Wessex. And it stood before a great pavilion, which was the court for the time, and where we should find the king waiting for us. There were several other tents joined to this great one, so that into them the king might retire; and there was a wide space, round which walked spearmen as sentries, between it and any other tent.

Some Devon thanes met us, and our men dismounted at the same time as we. Then Odda led us four to the door of the pavilion, and we were ushered in with much ceremony.

Inside the great tent was like a round hall, carpeted, and tapestry-hung in a way I had never seen before. There were many richly-dressed nobles present, and most of these were grouped round a high place over against the door, where I saw at once that the king sat on a throne in all state.

Now, coming from bright sunshine into the cool shadow of the place, I was dazzled at first; but Kolgrim's eyes were quick, and we had hardly crossed the threshold, if I might call it so, when he plucked at my cloak.

"Master," he whispered, "let me bide with the men; this is no place for me."

"Hush," I whispered; "the king is yonder."

"Ay, master--let me go--the king is Godred whom I jested with."

Harek was smiling, and he pulled Kolgrim forward.

"Have no fear," he said; "those who play bowls expect rubs."

Then the king came down from his throne and towards us. He had on gilded armour beneath his long, ermine-trimmed blue cloak, and that pleased me. He had sword and seax, but no helm, though that was on a table by the throne--for he wore a crown.

Then I too saw that Godred, as he called himself, was, as the scald had guessed rightly, the king, and I was a little angry that he had tricked me thus. But he was laughing at Kolgrim as he came, and my anger passed at once. King or thane, here was a pleasant greeting enough.

He held out his hand to Odda first and then to me. The Saxon kissed it, bending one knee, which was doubtless right for him, as owning allegiance thereto. But I shook hands in our own way, saying:

"Skoal to Alfred the king."

Which seemed to please him, for he answered:

"Welcome to King Ranald. I am glad my letter brought you. My counsellor, Godred, feared you might not care to come."

"The letter turned the scale, lord king," I said. "Yet I would have you remember what I said yesterday about my kingship."

"Ay, cousin, I mind it," he answered, laughing. "Also I mind that a king's son is a king's son, whatever else he may be called."

Then he shook hands with Harek, and after that turned to Kolgrim, holding out his hand also to him.

"Concerning sails," he said gravely, "I have many questions to ask you. Is it to the starboard hand that the bolt rope goes, or to the other board?"

"I pray you to forget my foolishness, lord king," cried Kolgrim, growing very red and shame faced.

"That I shall not," the king answered, laughing. "I owe you thanks for such a jest as I have not played on a man for many a long day. Truly I have been more light hearted for my laugh ever since."

"Ay, lord, you had the laugh of me," Kolgrim said, grinning uneasily.

Then the king nodded gaily to him and asked who Thord was.

"This is my master in sea craft," said Odda. "Verily I fear him as I have feared no man since I was at school. But he cured the seasickness of me."

"Maybe I forgot the sickness when I sent landsmen to sea in all haste," said the king. "Nevertheless, Thord, how fought they when blows were going?"

"Well enough, king. And I will say that what I tried to teach them they tried to learn," answered Thord.

"Wherein is hope. You think that I may have good seamen in time, therefore?"

"Ay, lord. It is in the blood of every man of our kin to take to the sea. They are like hen-bred ducklings now, and they do but want a duck to lead them pondwards. Then may hen cackle in vain for them."

The king laughed.

"Faith," he said, "I--the hen--drove Odda into the pond. He is, according to his own account, a poor duckling."

"Let him splash about a little longer, lord king," said Thord.

But Odda spoke with a long face.

"Not so, King Alfred, if you love me. Landsman am I, and chicken-hearted at sea. Keep the gamecock to mind the farmyard; there be more birds than ducks needed."

"Make a song hereof, Harek," said the king. "Here is word play enough for any scald."

Then sang Harek, laughing, and ever ready with verses:

> "The gamecock croweth bravely,
> And guardeth hawk-scared hen roost;
> But when the sea swan swimmeth

> Against the shoreward nestings,
> There mighty mallard flappeth,
> And frayeth him from foray;
> Yet shoreward if he winneth,
> The gamecock waits to meet him."

"That is in my favour," said Odda. "Mind you the scald's words, I pray you, lord king, and send me to my right place, even with hawk on one side and swan on the other."

So a pleasant laugh went round, and then the king went back to his throne, and spoke words of open thanks to us of the fleet who had gained him such victory. Good words they were, neither too few nor too many, such as would make every man who heard them long to hear the like of himself again.

Now, while he was speaking, men came to the tent door and waited for his words to end; and then one came forward and told a noble, who seemed to be ordering the state which was kept, that Danish lords had come to speak with the king.

It seemed that this was expected, for when he heard it, Alfred bade that they should be brought in.

There were six of them in all, and they were in handsome dresses, but without mail, though not unarmed. The leader of them was Jarl Osmund, whom I had seen for a moment in Wareham street. I thought that his handsome face was careworn, as though peace would be welcome to him. But he and all his comrades carried themselves bravely.

Now there was long converse between the king and these chiefs, and it seemed that peace would be made.

Yet Alfred's face was hard as he spoke to them--not like the bright looks with which he had jested with us just now, or the earnest kingly regard which had gone with his words of thanks.

Presently the Danes said that the whole force would retire into Mercia beyond Thames, harming none by the way, and keeping peace thereafter, if the conditions were honourable.

Then the king flashed out into scorn:

"What honour is to be looked for by oath breakers?"

"We are not oath breakers, King Alfred," Osmund said, looking him in the face.

"Once did the Danes swear to me on their holy ring, which seems to me to be their greatest oath, and they broke the peace so made. What is that but that they are forsworn?"

"We swore nought to you, lord king," Osmund said. "Half of the men with us came newly from across the sea but a week or so since. Guthrum and those who swore are in their own land."

Then the king glanced at me, suddenly, as it would seem, remembering what I had told him of the freedom of the chiefs.

"Ha! now I mind me of a word spoken in time," he said. "It has seemed to me that there was oath breaking; maybe I was wrong. I will take your words that you have not done so. Is that amends enough?"

"It is well said, lord king," Osmund answered gravely.

"But," Alfred went on, "I must have the word of every chief who is in Exeter, and they must speak for every man. Tell me in all truth if there are those who would not make peace with me?"

Then said Osmund:

"Some will not, but they are few."

"What if you make peace and they do not? what shall you do with them?"

"They must go their own way; we have no power over them."

"Has not Guthrum?"

"No more than we. A free Dane cannot be bound, unless he chooses, by another man's word."

Then Alfred said plainly:

"I cannot treat for peace till I have the word of every chief in Exeter. Go your ways and let that be known."

So Osmund bowed, and went out with his fellows. And when he had gone, the king turned to me.

"Have I spoken aright, King Ranald?"

"In the best way possible, lord king," I answered.

"Go after those Danish lords," the king said to one of his thanes, "and bid them to feast with me tonight, for I think that I have said too much to them."

So they were bidden to the king's feast presently, and I suppose they could do nought but come, for it was plain that he meant to honour them. After they had gone back into the town, Alfred spoke with my men, and what he said pleased them well.

Then he went to his resting tent, and I walked with Odda to his quarters, and sat there, waiting for the king to send for me to speak with him, as I expected. But word came that he would wait till he had heard more of the Danish answer to his message before we spoke together of that he had written of to me. So he prayed me to wait in the camp till he had seen the Danes again, and told Odda to find quarters for us.

"So we shall have a good talk together," the ealdorman said. "I am glad you are not going back to the ships yet."

So was I, for all this fresh life that I had not seen before pleased me. Most of all I wished to see more of Alfred and the state in which he lived.

Now, just when I was ready for the feast, and was sitting with Odda, there came a guard to the tent and said that the chief of the Danes was seeking King Ranald.

Then Odda said:

"What wills he? we have no traffic with Danes."

"He would speak with King Ranald," the man said.

Then said I:

"If it is Osmund the jarl, I think I know why he comes.--Let him come in here and speak before you, ealdorman."

"Why, do you know him?"

"I cannot rightly say that I do, but I nearly came to do so."

Then Odda wondered, and answered:

"Forgive me; one grows suspicious about these Danes. I will go hence, and you shall speak with him alone. Maybe he wants your word with the king, because you know the ways of the viking hosts."

"No," said I; "stay here. Whatever it is he has to say cannot be private; nor would I hear anything from him that you might not."

"As you will. Let him come here," Odda said; and the man went out.

Then entered Jarl Osmund, richly dressed for the king's feast, and he looked from one of us to the other as we rose to greet him. Suddenly he smiled grimly.

"I looked to find strangers, and was about to ask for King Ranald. However, Odda the ealdorman and I have met before, as I am certain."

"Faith, we have," said Odda. "Nor am I likely to forget it. It was at Ashdown fight."

"And elsewhere," said the jarl. "But it was ever fair fighting between us."

"Else had you slain me when I was down," said Odda frankly, and with a smile coming into his face.

"The score is even on that count," said Osmund, and with that, with one accord their hands met, and they laughed at each other.

That was good to see, and ever should things be so between brave foes and honest.

Then Osmund looked at me.

"Now have I met with two men whom I have longed to see," he said, "for you must be King Ranald Vemundsson. Two foes I have--if it must be so said--of whom I have nought but good to say."

"So," laughed Odda. "When fought you twain, and which let the other go?"

"We have not fought," the jarl answered. "But I have deeper reason for thanking Ranald than for sparing my own life, or for staying a blow in time out of sheer love of fair play."

Then he took my hand and looked me in the face.

"It was a good deed and noble that you wrought for me but the other day," he said earnestly. "I do not know how to thank you enough. My daughter laid command on me that I should seek you and tell you this; but indeed I needed no bidding when I heard how she escaped."

"I had been nidring had I not helped a lady in need," I said, being in want of better words.

"What is all this?" said Odda; for I had told him nought of the matter, not seeing any reason to do so.

Then Osmund must needs tell him of what Kolgrim and I had done; and the ealdorman laughed at me, though one might see that the affair pleased him.

"This king," he said, "having no kingdom of his own, as he says, goes about helping seasick ealdormen and lonely damsels, whereby he will end with more trouble on his hands than any kingdom would give him."

"I am only one," I said; "Kolgrim and Thord are in this also."

Then Osmund took a heavy gold bracelet from his arm.

"This is for Kolgrim, your comrade," he said, half doubtfully, "if I may give it him in remembrance of a brave deed well done. Will he be too proud to accept it?"

"I may give it him, certainly," I said, taking the gift.

Then Odda would not be behindhand, and he pulled off his own armlet.

"If Kolgrim is to be remembered, Thord will never be forgotten. Give this to him in sheer gratitude for swearing at me in such wise that he overcame the sore sickness that comes of the swaying of the deck that will not cease."

"Give it him yourself, ealdorman," I said. "You know him over well to send it by another. It would not be so good a gift."

"As you will," he answered. "But I fear that viking terribly. Black grows his face, and into his beard he blows, and the hard Norse words grumble like thunder from his lips. Then know I that Odda the ealdorman has been playing the land lubber again, and wonder what is wrong. Nor is it long ere I find out, and I and my luckless crew are flying to mind what orders are howled at us. In good truth, if Alfred ever needs me to hurry in aught, let him send Thord the viking to see that I do so. One may know how I fear him, since I chose rather to risk battle with Jarl Osmund on shore than to bide near him in my own ship any longer."

Then the jarl and I laughed till our sides ached, and Odda joined us when he could not help it, so doleful was his face and solemn were his words when he told his tale. But I knew that he and Thord were the best of friends after those few days in the ship together, and that the rough old viking had given every man of the crew confidence. Nevertheless he was apt to rage somewhat when things went in slovenly wise.

So Odda helped me through with Osmund's thanks, and I was glad. I was glad also that the horns blew for the feast, so that no more could be said about the Wareham doings.

Now I sat close to King Alfred at the feast, and saw much of his ways with men. I thought it plain that he had trouble at times in keeping back the pride and haughtiness which I had heard had been the fault in both Neot and himself, for now and then they showed plainly. Then he made haste to make amends if one was hurt by what he had said in haste. But altogether I thought him even more kingly than the mighty Harald Fairhair in some ways.

Truly he had not the vast strength and stature of Norway's king, but Alfred's was the kingliness of wisdom and statecraft.

Once I said to Odda:

"Can your king fight?"

"Ay, with head as well as with hand," he answered. "His skill in weapon play makes up for lack of weight and strength. He is maybe the best swordsman and spearman in England."

I looked again at him, and I saw that since last I turned my eyes on him he had grown pale, and now his face was drawn, and was whitening under some pain, as it would seem; and I gripped Odda's arm.

"See!" I said, "the king dies! he is poisoned!"

And I was starting up, but the ealdorman held me back.

"I pray you pay no heed," he said urgently. "It is the king's dark hour; he will be well anon."

But nevertheless Alfred swayed in his seat, and two young thanes who stood waiting on him came to either side and helped him up, and together they took him, tottering, into the smaller tent that opened behind the throne; while all the guests were silent, some in fear, like myself, but others looking pityingly only.

Then a tall man in a dress strange to me--a bishop, as I knew presently--rose up, and said to those who knew not what was the matter:

"Doubtless all know that our good king is troubled with a strange illness that falls on him from time to time. This is such a time. Have no fear therefore, for the pain he suffers will pass. He does not will that any should be less merry because of him."

So the feast went on, though the great empty chair seemed to damp the merriment sadly. I asked Odda if this trouble often befell the king.

"Ay, over often," he said, "and one knows not when it will come. No leech knows what it is, and all one can say is that it seems to harm him not at all when it has gone."

I asked no more, but the king did not come back to the feast, as he would at times when things happened thus. It seemed that often the trouble fell on him when feasting, and some have said that it was sent to prevent him becoming over proud, at his own prayer [viii].

Soon the Danes rose up, and would go. Some of the great thanes set them forth with all honour, and the feast ended. There was no long sitting over the wine cup at Alfred's board, though none could complain that he stinted them.

Then the tall bishop who had spoken just now came to me.

"The king will speak with you now, King Ranald, if you will come," he said.

So I went with him, and Odda came also. The king was lying on a couch without his heavy state robes, and when we entered the small tent the attendants left him. He was very pale, but the pain seemed to have gone, and he looked up pleasantly at me.

"My people are used to this, cousin," he said, "but I fear I put you out sorely."

"I thought you poisoned," I said; "but Odda told me not to fear."

"Ay, that has been the thought of others before this," he said. "Have you ever seen the like in any man? I ask every stranger, in hopes that I may hear of relief."

"No, I have not, lord king," I answered; "but I can grave runes that will, as I think, keep away such pain if you bear them on you. Thord, whom you know, taught me them. Maybe it would be better for him to grave them, for runes wrongly written are worse than none, and these are very powerful."

"That is a kindly thought, cousin," Alfred answered; "but I am sure that no runes will avail when the prayers of my people, from holy Neot to the little village children, do not. And I fear that even would they heal me, I must sooner bear the pain than seek to magic spells."

"Nay, but try them, King Alfred," I said; "there is no ill magic in them."

Now he saw that I was in earnest, and put me by very kindly.

"I must ask Sigehelm, our bishop here, who is my best leech next to Neot.

"What say you, father?"

"Even as you have said, my king."

"Maybe, bishop," said I, "you have never tried the might of runes?"

Whereat the good man held up his hands in horror, making no answer, and I laughed a little at him.

"Well, then," said the king, "we will ask Neot, for mostly he seems to say exactly what I do not."

"Neot has gone to Cornwall, and I had forgotten to give you that message from him. He says he will be there for a time," I said, rather ashamed at having let slip the message from my mind.

"So you saw him?" said Alfred.

"I knew he went to the ships yesterday after Godred came back," he added, laughing.

"He read my letter for me, and after that I had a good deal of talk with him," I said.

"Then," said Sigehelm, "you have spoken with the best man in all our land."

Now the king said that he would let the question of the runes, for which he thanked me, stand over thus; and then he asked me to sit down and hear what he would ask me to do for him, if I had no plans already made for myself.

I said that I had nothing so certainly planned but that I and my men would gladly serve him.

"Then," he said, "I would ask you to winter with me, and set my ships in order. There will be work for you and all your men, for you shall give them such command in any ship of mine as you know they are best fitted for. I would ask you to help me carry out that plan of which you spoke to me when I was Godred."

When Odda heard that, he rubbed his hands together, saying:

"Ay, lord king, you have found the right man at last."

"Then in the spring you shall take full command of the fleet we will build and the men we shall raise; and you shall keep the seas for me, if by that time we know that we can work well together."

He looked hard at me, waiting my answer.

"Lord king," I said at last, "this is a great charge, and they say that I am always thought older than I am, being given at least five winters beyond the two-and-twenty that I have seen;" for I thought it likely that the king held that I had seen more than I had.

"I was but twenty when I came to the throne," he answered. "I have no fear for you. More than his best I do not look for from any man; nor do I wonder if a man makes mistakes, having done so many times myself."

Here Sigehelm made some sign to the king, to which he paid no heed at the time, but went on:

"As for your men, I will give them the same pay that Harald of Norway gives to his seamen, each as you may choose to rank them for me. You may know what that is."

"Harek the scald knows," I said. "They will be well pleased, for the pay is good, and places among Harald's courtmen are much sought for."

Then Alfred smiled, and spoke of myself.

"As for King Ranald himself, he will be my guest."

"I am a wandering viking, and I seem to have found great honour," I said. "What I can do I will, in this matter. Yet there is one thing I must say, King Alfred. I would not be where men are jealous of me."

"The only man likely to be so is Odda," the king answered. "You must settle that with him. It is the place that he must have held that you are taking. No man in all England can be jealous of a viking whose business is with ships. But Odda put this into my mind at first, and then Godred found out that he was right."

"Lord king," said I, "had I known who you were at that time, I should have spoken no differently. We Northmen are free in speech as in action."

"So says Odda," replied Alfred, smiling. "He has piteous tales of one Thord, whom you sent to teach him things, and the way in which he was made to learn."

"Nevertheless," said Odda, "I will not have Thord blamed, for it is in my mind that we should have learned in no other way so quickly."

Again the bishop signed to the king, and Alfred became grave.

"Here is one thing that our good Sigehelm minds me of. It seems that you are a heathen."

"Why, no, if that means one who hates Christians," I said. "Certainly I do not do that, having no cause to do so. Those whom I know are yourself, and Neot, and Odda, and one or two more only."

"That is not it," said the king. "What we call a heathen is one who worships the old gods--the Asir."

"Certainly I do that--ill enough."

"Then," said Alfred, while Odda shifted in his seat, seeming anxious as to how I should take this, "it is our rule that before a heathen man can serve with us, he shall at least be ready to learn our faith, and also must be signed with the cross, in token that he hates it not [lviii]."

"Why should I not learn of your faith?" I said. "Neot asked me of mine. As for the other, I do not know rightly what it means. I see your people sign themselves crosswise, and I cannot tell why, unless it is as we hallow a feast by signing it with Thor's hammer."

"It is more than that," Alfred said, motioning to Sigehelm to say nothing, for he was going to speak. "First you must know what it means, and then say if you will be signed therewith."

Then he said to Sigehelm:

"Here is one who will listen to good words, not already set against them, as some Danes are, by reason of ill report and the lives of bad Christians. Have no fear of telling him what you will."

Now, if I were to serve King Alfred, it seemed to me to be only reasonable that I should know the beliefs of those with whom I had to do. Then I minded me of Neot, and his way of asking about my gods, as if the belief of every man was of interest to him.

"Here is a deep matter to be talked of, King Alfred," I said. "It does not do to speak lightly and carelessly of such things. Nor am I more than your guest as yet, willing to hear what you would have me know. When winter has gone, and you know if I shall be any good to you, then will be question if I enter your service altogether, and by that time I shall know enough. Maybe I shall see Neot again; he and I began to speak of these things."

Then Sigehelm said:

"I think this is right, and Neot can tell you more in a few words than I in many. Yet whatever you ask me I will try to tell you."

"I want to speak with Neot," answered the king, "and we will ride together and seek him when peace is made. I have many things to say to him and ask him. We will go as soon as it is safe."

So ended my talk with King Alfred at that time, and I was well content therewith. So also were my men, for it was certain that every one of them would find some place of command, were it but over a watch, when Alfred's new sea levies were to be trained.

Many noble Saxons I met in the week before peace was made with the Danes in Exeter, for all the best were gathered there. Most of all I liked Ethered, the young ealdorman of Mercia, and Ethelnoth, the Somerset ealdorman, and Heregar, the king's standard bearer, an older warrior, who had seen every battle south of Thames since the long ago day when Eahlstan the bishop taught his flock how to fight for their land against the heathen.

These were very friendly with me, and I should see more of them if I were indeed to ward the Wessex coasts, and for that reason they made the more of me.

Now I saw no more of Osmund the jarl, for Odda knew that the lesser folk would mistrust me if I had any doings with the Danes. Maybe I was sorry not to see the Lady Thora; but if I had seen her, I do not know what I should have said to her, having had no experience of ladies' ways at any time, which would have made me seem foolish perhaps.

Chapter VII. The Pixies' Dance.

I do not know that there is anything more pleasant after long weeks at sea than to have a good horse under one, and to be riding in the fresh winds of early autumn over new country that is beautiful in sunlight. So when at last every Danish chief had made submission, and the whole host had marched back to what they held as their own land in Mercia, going to Gloucester, as was said, with Odda and Ethered the ealdormen hanging on their rear with a great levy, I rode with King Alfred to find Neot his cousin gaily enough. Thord stayed with the ships, but the scald and Kolgrim were with me, and the king mounted us well. Ethelnoth of Somerset came also, and some forty men of the king's household; and all went armed, for the country we had to cross was of the wildest, though we went by the great road that runs from west to east of England, made even before the Romans came. But it crossed the edge of Dartmoor, the most desolate place in all the land, where outlaws and masterless men found fastnesses whence none could drive them.

One could not wish for a more pleasant companion than Alfred, and the miles went easily. We had both hawks and hounds with us, for there was game in plenty, and the king said that with the ending of the war, and the beginning of new hopes for his fleet, he would cast care aside for a little. So he was joyous and free in speech, and at times he would sing in lightness of heart, and would bid Harek sing also, so that it was pleasant to hear them. Ever does Harek say that no man sings better than Alfred of England.

In late afternoon we came to the wild fringe of Dartmoor, and here the king had a guest house in a little village which he was wont to use on these journeys to see Neot. We should rest there, and so cross the wastes in full daylight. So he went in, maybe fearing his sickness, which was indeed a sore burden to him, though he was wont to make light of it; but Ethelnoth asked me if we should not spend the hours of evening light in coursing a bustard or two, for many were about the moorland close at hand. They would be welcome at the king's table, he said; and I, fresh from the sea and camp, asked for nothing better than a good gallop over the wide-stretching hillsides.

So we took fresh horses from those that were led for us, and rode away. We took hawks--the king had given me a good one when we started, for a Saxon noble ever rides with hawk on wrist--and two leash of greyhounds.

I was for putting my arms aside, but the ealdorman said it was better not to do so, by reason of the moor folk, who were wild enough to fall on a small party at times. It was of little moment, however; for we rode in the lighter buff jerkins instead of heavy mail, and were not going far.

Ethelnoth took two men with him, and my two comrades were with me--Kolgrim leading the hounds in leash beside his horse. We went across the first hillside, and from its top looked northward and westward as far as one could see over the strange grey wastes of the moorland.

Then from the heather almost under our feet rose a great bustard that ran down wind with outstretched wings before us, seeking the lonelier country. Kolgrim whooped, and slipped the leash, and the hounds sprang after it, and we followed cheering. It was good to feel the rush of hillside air in our faces, and the spring and stretch of the horses under us, and to see the long-reached hounds straining after the great bird that might well be able to escape them.

I suppose that Ethelnoth started a second bird. I did not look behind me to see what any man was doing, but followed the chase round the spur of a granite-topped hillside, and forgot him. For when the bustard took wing for a heavy flight, and lit and ran again, and again flew with wings that failed each time more and more, while the strong legs were the stronger for the short rest, and when the good hounds were straining after it, one could not expect me to care for aught but that.

It had been strange if I thought of anything but the sport. I knew there were two horsemen close by, a little wide on either flank, but behind me. So we took the bird after a good chase, and then I knew that we had in some way shaken off the Saxons, and that we three vikings were together. It did not trouble us, for one looks for such partings, and Ethelnoth had his own bounds. So we went on, and found another bustard, and took it.

"Now we must go back," I said; "one must have a thought for the king's horses."

So we turned, and then a heron rose from a boggy stream below us, and that was a quarry not to be let go. I unhooded the falcon and cast her off, and straightway forgot everything but the most wonderful sight that the field and forest can give us--the dizzy upward climbing circles of hawk and heron, who strive to gain the highest place cloudwards, one for attack, the other for safety.

The evening sunlight flashed red from the bright under feathers of the strong wings as the birds swung into it from the shadow of the westward hill, and still they soared, drifting westward with the wind over our heads. Then with a great rushing sound the heron gave up, and fell, stone-like, from the falcon that had won to air above him at last. At once the long wings of his enemy closed halfway, and she swooped after him.

Then back and up, like a sword drawn at need, went the heron's sharp beak; and the falcon saw it, and swerved and shot past her nearly-taken prey. Again the heron began to tower up and up with a harsh croak that seemed like a cry of mockery; then the wondrous swing and sweep of the long, tireless wings of the passage hawk, and the cry of another heron far off, scared by its fellow's note; and again for us a canter over the moorland, eye and hand and knee together wary for both hawk above and good horse below, till the falcon bound to the heron, and both came to the ground, and there was an end in the grey shadow of the Dartmoor tors. Ay, but King Alfred's hawk was a good one!

"Now, where shall we seek Ethelnoth?" I said.

"No good seeking him," said Harek. "We had better make our way back to the village."

We coupled up the greyhounds again and hooded the falcon, and rode leisurely back over our tracks for some way. The sun set about that time into a purple bank of mist beyond the farther hills. One does not note how the miles go when one finds sport such as this, and presently we began to be sure that we had ridden farther than we had thought. We knew, as we thought, the direction from which we had come, and steered, sailor-wise, by the sunset. But we could take no straight course because of the hills, and we were as often off the line as on.

Then crept up the mist from the valleys, and we had nought to steer by, for the wind dropped. Then I said:

"Let the horses take us home; they know better than we."

So we rode on slowly until darkness came, but never saw so much as a light that might guide us. And presently we let the dogs loose, thinking that they would go homewards. But a greyhound is not like a mastiff, and they hung round us, careless, or helpless, in the mists and darkness.

Presently we came to a place where the horses stopped of their own accord. There was a sheer rock on one side, and the hill was steep below us, and a stream brawled somewhere before us.

"Well," I said, "here we stay for the night. It is of no use wandering any longer, and the night is warm."

We thought nothing of this, for any hunter knows that such a chance may befall him in a strange and wild country. So we laughed together and off-saddled and hobbled the horses, and so sat down supperless to wait for morning under the rock. The mist was clammy round us, thinning and then thickening again as the breaths of wind took it; but the moon would rise soon, and then maybe it would go.

We had no means of making a fire, and no cloaks; so sleep came hardly, and we talked long. Then the dogs grew uneasy, and presently wandered away into the fog and darkness. I thought that perhaps they heard some game stirring, and did not wonder at them.

Now I was just sleeping, when I heard the sharp yelp of a dog in pain, and sat up suddenly. Then came a second, and after that the distant sound of voices that rose for a moment and hushed again.

"We must be close to the village after all," I said, for my comrades were listening also; "but why did the hounds yell like that?"

"Some old dame has taken the broomstick to them," said Kolgrim. "They are hungry, and have put their noses into her milk pails."

"It is too late for open doors," I said; "unless they have found our own lodging, where some are waiting for us. But there they would not be beaten."

"Ho!" said Kolgrim, in another minute or so, "yonder is a fire."

The wind had come round the hillside and swept the mist away for a moment, and below us in the valley was a speck of red light that made a wide glow in the denser fog that hung there. One could hardly say how far off it was, for fog of any sort confuses distance; but the brook seemed to run in the direction of the fire, and it was likely that any house stood near its banks.

"Let us follow the brook and see what we can find," I said therefore. "These mists are chill, and I will confess that I am hungry. We cannot lose our way if we keep to the water, and the horses will be safe enough."

Anything was better, as it seemed to us, than trying to think that we slept comfortably here, and so we rose up and went down the banks of the stream at once; and the way proved to be easy enough, if rocky. The bank on this side was higher, and dry therefore, so that we had no bogs to fear. We knew enough of them in the Orkneys and on the Sutherland coast.

The white mist grew very thick, but the firelight glow grew redder as we went on, and at last we came near enough to hear many voices plainly; but presently, when one shouted, we found that the tongue was not known to us.

"Now it is plain whom we have come across," I said. "This is a camp of the Cornish tin traders, of whom the king told us. They are honest folk enough, and will put us on the great road. They must be close to it."

That seemed so likely that we left the brook and began to draw nearer to the fire, the voices growing plainer every moment, though we could see no man as yet.

Now, all of a sudden, every voice was silent, and we stopped, thinking we were heard perhaps; though it did seem strange to me that no dogs were about a camp of traders. I was just about to call out that we were friends, when there began a low, even beating, as of a drum of some sort, and then suddenly a wild howl that sounded like a war cry of maddened men, and after that a measured tramping of feet that went swiftly and in time to a chant, the like of which I had never heard before, and which made me grasp Harek by the arm.

"What, in Odin's name, is this?" r said, whispering.

"Somewhat uncanny," answered the scald. "Let us get back to the horses and leave this place."

Then we turned back, and Kolgrim's foot lit on a stone that rolled from under it, and he fell heavily with a clatter of weapons on the scattered rocks of the stream bank.

There was a howl from the firelight, and the chanting stopped, and voices cried in the uncouth tongue angrily, and there came a pattering of unshod feet round us in the thickness, with a word or two that seemed as if of command, and then silence, but for stealthy footfalls drawing nearer to us. And I liked it not.

We pulled Kolgrim up, and went on upstream, drawing our swords, though I yet thought of nothing but tin merchants whom we had disturbed in some strange play of their own. Doubtless they would take us for outlaws.

Now through the fog, dark against the flickering glow of the fire, and only seen against it, came creeping figures; and I suppose that some dull glitter of steel from helms or sword hilts betrayed us to them, for word was muttered among them, and the rattle of stones shifted by bare feet seemed to be all round us. I thought it time to speak to them.

"We are friends, good people," I said. "We mean no harm, and have but lost our way."

There was a whistle, and in a moment the leaping shadows were on us. Kolgrim went down under a heavy blow on his helm, and lay motionless; and Harek was whirled by a dozen pairs of hands off his feet, and fell heavily with his foes upon him. I slew one, or thought I slew him, and I stood over Kolgrim and kept them back with long sword sweeps, crying to them to hold, for we were friends--King Alfred's guests.

Now they were yelling to one another, and one threw a long-noosed line over me from behind. It fell over my arms, and at once they drew it tight, jerking me off my feet. As I went down, a howling crowd fell on me and took the good sword from me, and bound me hand and foot, having overpowered me by sheer numbers.

Then they looked at Kolgrim, and laughed, and left him. I was sure he was dead then, and I fell into a great dumb rage that seemed like to choke me.

They dragged the scald and me to the fire, and I saw into what hands we had fallen, and I will say that I was fairly afraid. For these were no thrifty Cornish folk, but wild-looking men, black haired and bearded, clad in skins of wolf, and badger, and deer, and sheep, with savage-eyed faces, and rough weapons of rusted iron and bronze and stone. So strange were their looks and terrible in the red light of the great fire, that I cried to Harek:

"These be trolls, scald! Sing the verses that have power to scare them."

Now it says much for Harek's courage that at once he lifted up no trembling voice and sang lustily, roaring verses old as Odin himself, such as no troll can abide within hearing of, so that those who bore him fell back amazed, and stared at him. Then I saw that on the arms and necks of one or two of these weird folk were golden rings flashing, and I saw, too, that our poor greyhounds lay dead near where I was, and I feared the more for ourselves.

But they did not melt away or fly before the spells that Harek hurled at them.

"These be mortal men," he said at last, "else had they fled ere now."

By this time they had left me, helpless as a log, and were standing round us in a sort of ring, talking together of slaying us, as I thought. I mind that the flint-tipped spears seemed cruel weapons. At last one of them said somewhat that pleased the rest, for they broke into a great laugh and clapped their hands.

"Here is a word I can understand," said Harek, "and that is 'pixies.'"

But I was looking to see where our swords were, and I saw a man take them beyond the fire and set them on what seemed a bank, some yards from it. Then they went to the scald and began to loosen his bonds, laughing the while.

"Have a care, Harek," I cried. "Make a rush for the swords beyond the fire so soon as you are free."

"I am likely to be hove into the said fire," said the scald, very coolly. "Howbeit I see the place where they are."

Then he gave a great bound and shout: but the numbers round him were too great, and they had him down again, and yet he struggled. This was sport to these savages, and those who were not wrestling with him leaped and yelled with delight to see it. And I wrestled and tore at my bonds; but they were of rawhide, and I could do nothing.

Then Harek said, breathing heavily:

"No good; their arms are like steel about me."

Then some came and dragged me back a little, and set me up sitting against a great stone, so I could see all that went on. Now I counted fifty men, and there were no women that I could see anywhere. Half of these were making a great ring with joined hands round the fire, and some piled more fuel on it--turf and branches of dwarf oak trees--and others sat round, watching the dozen or so that minded Harek. One sat cross-legged near me, with a great pot covered tightly with skin held between his knees.

Next they set Harek on his feet, and led him to the ring round the fire. Two of the men--and they were among the strongest of all--loosened their hands, and each gripped the scald by the wrist and yelled aloud, and at once the man beat on the great pot's cover drum-wise, and the ring of men whirled away round the fire in the wild dance whose foot beats we had heard as we came. Then those who sat round raised the chant we heard also.

I saw Harek struggle and try to break away; but at that they whirled yet more quickly, and he lost his footing, and fell, and was dragged up; and then he too must dance, or be haled along the ground. My eyes grew dizzy with watching, while the drum and the chant dulled into a humming in my brain.

"This cannot go on for long," I thought.

But then, from among those who sat round and chanted, I saw now one and now another dart to the ring and take the place of a dancer who seemed to tire; and so at last one came and gripped Harek's wrist and swung into the place of his first holder before he knew that any change was coming, and so with the one on the other side of him.

Then it was plain that my comrade must needs fall worn out before long, and I knew what I was looking on at. It was the dance of the pixies, in truth--the dance that ends but with the death of him who has broken in on their revels--and I would that I and Harek had been slain rather with Kolgrim by the stream yonder.

At last the scald fell, and then with a great howl they let him go, flinging him out of the circle like a stone, and he lay in a heap where they tossed him, and was quite still.

Then the dancers raised a shout, and came and sat down, and some brought earthen vessels of drink to refresh them, while they began to turn their eyes to me, whose turn came next.

Whereon a thought came into my mind, and I almost laughed, for a hope seemed to lie in a simple trick enough. That I would try presently.

Now I looked, and hoped to see Harek come to himself; but he did not stir. He lay near the swords, and for the first time now, because of some thinning of the mist, I saw what was on the bank where these had been placed. There was a great stone dolmen, as they call it--a giant house, as it were, made of three flat stones for walls, and a fourth for a roof, so heavy that none know how such are raised nowadays. They might have served for a table, or maybe a stool, for a Jotun. The two side walls came together from the back, so that the doorway was narrow; and a man might stand and keep it against a dozen, for it was ten feet high, and there was room for sword play. One minds all these things when they are of no use to him, and only the wish that they could be used is left. Nevertheless, as I say, I had one little hope.

It was not long before the savage folk were ready for my dance, and they made the ring again, refreshed. The drum was taken up once more, and a dozen men came and unbound me. I also struggled as Harek had struggled, unavailingly. When I was quiet they led me to the circle, and I watched for my plan to work.

When I was within reach of the two who should hold me, I held out my hands to grasp theirs, without waiting for them to seize me. The man on my right took my wrist in a grasp like steel; but the other was tricked, and took my hand naturally enough. Whereat my heart leaped.

"Now will one know what a grip on the mainsheet is like!" I thought; and even as the hand closed there came the yell, and the thud of the earthen drum, and I was whirled away.

Now I kept going, for my great fear was that I should grow dizzy quickly. I was taller than any man in the ring, and once I found out the measure of the chant I went on easily, keeping my eyes on the man ahead of me. That was the one to my right; for they went against the sun, which is an unlucky thing to do at any time.

Once we went round, and I saw the great dolmen and the gleam of sword Helmbiter beneath it. Then it was across the fire, and again I passed it. I could not choose my place, as it seemed, and suddenly with all my force I gripped the hand I held and around the bones of it together, so that no answering grip could come. In a moment the man let go of his fellow with the other hand, and screamed aloud, and cast himself on the ground, staying the dance, so that those after him fell over us. I let go, and swung round and smote my other holder across the face; and he too let go, and I was free, and in the uproar the dancers knew not what had happened. Smiting and kicking, I got clear of them, and saw that the dolmen towered across the fire, and straightway I knew that through the smoke was the only way. I leaped at it, and cleared it fairly, felling a man on the other side as I did so.

Then I had Helmbiter in my hand, and I shouted, and stepped back to the narrow door of the dolmen, and there stood, while the wild men gathered in a ring and howled at me. One ran and brought the long line that had noosed me before, but the stone doorway protected me from that; and one or two hurled spears at me, clumsily enough for me to ward them off.

So we stood and watched each other, and I thought they would make a rush on me. Harek lay within sweep of my sword, and his weapon was nearer them than me, and one of them picked it up and went to plunge it in him.

Then I stepped out and cut that man down, and the rest huddled back a little at my onslaught. Whereon I drew my comrade back to my feet, lest they should bring me out again and noose me.

As I did that, the one who seemed to be the chief leaped at me, club in air; but I was watching for him, and he too fell, and I shouted, to scare back the rest.

There was an answering shout, and Kolgrim, with the Berserker fury on him, was among the wild crowd from out of the darkness, and his great sword was cutting a way to my side.

Then they did not stay for my sword to be upon them also, but they fled yelling and terror stricken, seeming to melt into the mist. In two minutes the firelit circle was quiet and deserted, save for those who had fallen; and my comrade and I stared in each other's faces in the firelight.

"Comrade," I cried in gladness, "I thought you were slain."

"The good helm saved me," he answered; "but I came round in time. What are these whom we have fought?"

I suppose the fury kept him up so far, for now I saw that his face was ashy pale, and his knees shook under him.

"Are you badly hurt?" I asked.

"My head swims yet--that is all. Where is the scald?"

I turned to him and pointed. Kolgrim sat down beside him and bent over him, leaning against the stone of the great dolmen.

"I do not think he is dead, master," he said. "Let us draw him inside this house, and then he will be safe till daylight--unless the trolls come back and we cannot hold this doorway till the sun rises."

"They are men, not trolls," I said, pointing to the slain who lay between us and the fire in a lane where Kolgrim had charged through them, "else had we not slain them thus."

"One knows not what Sigurd's sword will not bite," he said.

"Why, most of that is your doing," I said, laughing a little.

But he looked puzzled, and shook his head.

"I mind leaping among them, but not that I slew any."

Now I thought that he would be the better for food. There had been plenty of both food and drink going among these wild people, whatever they were, and they had not waited to take anything. So I said I would walk round the fire and see what I could find, and went before he could stay me.

I had not far to go either, for there were plentiful remains of a roasted sheep or two set aside with the skins, and alongside them a pot of heather ale; so that we had a good meal, sitting in the door of the dolmen, while the moon rose. But first we tried to make Harek drink of the strong ale. He was beginning to breathe heavily now, and I thought he would come round presently. Whether he had been hurt by the whirling of the dance or by the fall when they cast him aside, I could not tell, and we could do no more for him.

"Sleep, master," said Kolgrim, when we had supped well; "I will watch for a time."

And he would have it so, and I, seeing that he was refreshed, was glad to lie down and sleep inside the dolmen, bidding him wake me in two hours and rest in turn.

But he did not. It was daylight when I woke, and the first ray of the sun came straight into the narrow doorway and woke me. And it waked Harek also. Kolgrim sat yet in the door with his sword across his knees.

"Ho, scald!" I said, "you have had a great sleep."

"Ay, and a bad dream also," he answered, "if dream it was."

For now he saw before us the burnt-out fire, and the slain, and the strangely-trampled circle of the dance.

"No dream, therefore," he said. "Is it true that I was made to dance round yon fire till I was nigh dead?"

"True enough. I danced also in turn," I said.

And then I told him how things had gone after his fall.

"Kolgrim has fought, therefore, a matter of fifty trolls," I said; "which is more than most folk can say for themselves."

Whereat he growled from the doorway:

"Maybe I was too much feared to know what I was doing."

We laughed at him, but he would have it so; and then we ate and drank, and spoke of going to where we had left the horses, being none so sure that we should find them at all.

Now the sun drank up the mists, and they cleared suddenly; and when the last wreaths fled up the hillsides and passed, we saw that the horses yet fed quietly where we had left them, full half a mile away up the steep rise down which the stream came.

And it was strange to see what manner of place this was in daylight, for until the mist lifted we could not tell in the least, and it was confused to us. Now all the hillsides glowed purple with heather in a great cup round us, and we were on a little rise in the midst of them whereon stood the dolmen, and the same hands doubtless that raised it had set up a wide circle of standing stones round about it, such as I have seen in the Orkneys. It was not a place where one would choose to spend the night.

There was no sign of the wild folk anywhere outside the stone circle. They had gone, and there seemed no cover for them anywhere, unless they dwelt in clefts and caves of the bare tors around us. So we feared no longer lest there should be any ambush set for us, and went about to see what they had left.

There were the long line that had noosed me, the earthen drum with its dry skin head, the raw hide thongs we had been bound with, and the food and drink; and that was all save what weapons lay round the slain, and the bodies of the two good greyhounds.

"These are but men, and not trolls as one might well think," I said, looking on those who lay before us.

One whom I had slain had a heavy gold torque round his neck, and twisted gold armlets, being the chief, as I think. Kolgrim took these off and gave them to me, and then he went to the drum and dashed it on a stone and broke it, saying nothing.

"Let us be going," I said. "These folk will come back and see to their dead."

But Kolgrim looked at the drumhead and took it, and then coiled the long line on his arm.

"Trust a sailor for never losing a chance of getting a new bit of rigging," said Harek, laughing; for he seemed none the worse for the things of last night, which indeed began to seem ghostly and dreamlike to us all. "But what good is the bit of skin?"

"Here be strange charms wrought into it," Kolgrim said. "It will make a sword scabbard that will avail somewhat against such like folk if ever we meet them again."

Truly there were marks as of branded signs on the bit of skin, and so he kept it; and I hung the gold trophies in my belt, and Harek took some of the remains of our supper: and so we went to the horses, seeing nothing of the wild men anywhere.

Very glad were the good steeds to see us come, and the falcon, who still sat on the saddle where I had perched her, spread her wings and ruffled her feathers to hear us. I unhooded and fed her; and we washed in the stream, and set out gaily enough, making southward, for so we thought we should strike the great road. And at last, when we saw its white line far off from a steep hillside, I was glad enough.

I cannot tell how we had reached our halting place through the hills in the dark, nor could I find it again directly. It was midday before we reached the road, riding easily; so that, what with the swift gallop of the hunting and the long hours of riding in mist and darkness, we had covered many miles. We saw no house till we were close to the road, and then lit on one made of stones and turf hard by it, where an old woman told us that no party had been by since daylight.

So we turned eastward and rode to meet the king, and did so before long. He had left men at his village to wait for us in case we came back there; but he laughed at us for losing ourselves, though he said he had no fear for sailors adrift in the wilds when Ethelnoth came in without us.

But when, as we rode on, I told him what had befallen us, he listened gravely, and at last said:

"I have heard the like of this before. Men say that the pixies dwell in the moorland, and will dance to death those who disturb them. What think you of those you have seen?"

I said that, having slain them, one could not doubt that they were men, if strange ones.

"That is what I think," he answered. "They are men who would be thought pixies. Maybe they are the pixies. I believe they are the last of the old Welsh folk who have dwelt in these wilds since the coming of the Romans or before. There were the like in the great fens of East Anglia and Mercia when Guthlac the Holy went there, and he thought them devils. None can reach these men or know where they dwell. Maybe they are heathen, and their dance in that stone ring was some unholy rite that you have seen. But you have been very far into the wastes, and I have never seen those stones."

And when he handled the gold rings, he showed me that they were very old; but when he handled the drumhead and looked at the marks thereon, he laughed.

"Here is the magic of an honest franklin's cattle brand. I have seen it on beasts about the hills before now. The pixies have made a raid on the farmer's herds at some time."

Now I think that King Alfred was right, and that we had fallen into the hands of wild Welsh or Cornish moor folk. But one should hear Kolgrim's tale of the matter as he shows his sword sheath that he made of the drumhead; for nothing would persuade him that it was not of more than mortal work.

"Had the good king been in that place with us, he would have told a different tale altogether," he says.

So we went on our journey quietly, and ever as we went and spoke with Alfred, I began to be sure that this pale and troubled king was the most wondrous man that I had ever seen. And now, as I look back and remember, I know that in many ways he was showing me that the faith he held shaped his life to that which seemed best in him to my eyes.

I know this, that had he scoffed at the Asir, I had listened to Neot not at all. But when we came to his place, I was ready, and more than ready, to hear what he had to tell me.

Chapter VIII. The Black Twelfth-Night.

When we came to the little out of the way village among the Cornish hills near which Neot, the king's cousin, had his dwelling, I thought it strange that any one should be willing to give up the stirring life at court for such a place as this. Here was only one fair-sized house in the place, and that was built not long before by the king for his own use when he came here, which was often. And Neot's own dwelling was but a little stone-walled and turf-roofed hut, apart from all others, on the hillside, and he dwelt there with one companion--another holy man, named Guerir, a Welshman by birth--content with the simple food that the villagers could give him, and spending his days in prayer and thought for the king and people and land that he loved.

But presently, as I came to know more of Neot, it seemed good that some should live thus in quiet while war and unrest were over the country, else had all learning and deeper thought passed away. It is certain from all that I have heard, from the king himself and from others, that without Neot's steady counsel and gathered wisdom Alfred had remained haughty and proud, well-nigh hated by his people, as he had been when first he came to the throne.

At one time he would drive away any who came to him with plaints or tales of wrong and trouble; but Neot spoke to him in such wise that he framed his ways differently. And now I used to wonder to see him stay and listen patiently to some rambling words of trifling want, told by a wayside thrall, to which it seemed below his rank to hearken, and next I would know that it was thus he made his people love him as no other king has been loved maybe. There was no man who could not win hearing from him now.

It is said of him that when Neot showed him the faults in his ways, he asked that some sickness, one that might not make him useless or loathsome to his people, might be sent him to mind him against his pride, and that so he had at first one manner of pain, and now this which I had seen. It may be so, for I know well that so he made it good for him, and he bore it most patiently. Moreover, I have never heard that it troubled him in the times of direst need, though the fear of it was with him always.

Now what Alfred and Neot spoke of at this time I cannot say, except that it was certainly some plan for the good of the land. I and my comrades hunted and hawked day by day until the evening came, and then would sup plainly with the king, and then sit at Neot's door in the warm evening, and talk together till the stars came out.

Many things we spoke of, and Neot told me what I would. I cannot write down those talks, though I mind every word of them. But there was never any talk of the runes I had offered.

Neot spoke mostly, but Alfred put in words now and then that ever seemed to make things plainer; and I mind how Ethelnoth the ealdorman sat silent, listening to questions and answers that maybe he had never needed to put or hear concerning his own faith.

At first I was only asking because the king wished it, then because I grew curious, and because I thought it well to know what a Saxon's faith was if I was to bide among Alfred's folk. Kolgrim listened, saying nought. But presently Harek the scald would ask more than I, and his questions were very deep, and I thought that as days went on he grew thoughtful and silent.

Then one evening the song woke within the scald's breast, and he said to Neot:

"Many and wise words have you spoken, Father Neot. Hear now the song of Odin--the Havamal--and tell me if you have aught to equal it."

"Sing, my son," the good man answered. "Wisdom is from above, and is taught in many ways."

Then Harek sang, and his voice went over the hillsides, echoing wonderfully; while we who heard him were very still, unwilling to lose one word or note of the song. Many verses and sayings of the "Havamal" I knew, but I had not heard it all before. Now it seemed to me that no more wisdom than is therein could be found [ix].

So when Harek ended Neot smiled on him, and said:

"That is a wondrous song, and I could have listened longer. There is little therein that one may not be wiser in remembering."

"There is nought wiser; it is Odin's wisdom," said Harek.

Now the old hermit, Guerir, Neot's friend, sat on the stone bench beside the king, and he said:

"Hear the words of the bards, the wondrous 'triads' of old time."

And he chanted them in a strange melody, unlike aught I had ever heard. And they, the old sayings, were wise as the "Havamal" itself. But he stopped ere long, saying:

"The English words will not frame the meaning rightly. I do no justice to the wisdom that is hidden."

Then Neot turned to the king, and said:

"Sing to Harek words from the book of Wisdom that we know. I think you can remember it well."

"I have not rhymed it," the king answered; "but sometimes the song shapes itself when it is needed."

He took Guerir's little harp and tuned it afresh and sang. And in the words were more wisdom than in the Havamal or in the song of the bards, so that I wondered; and Harek was silent, looking out to the sunset with wide eyes.

Not long did the king sing, as it seemed to us; and when he ceased, Harek made no sign.

"Sing now, my cousin, words that are wiser than those; even sing from the songs of David the king."

So said Neot; and Alfred sang again very wondrously, and as with some strange awe of the words he said. Then to me it seemed that beside these the words of Odin were as nought. They became as words of the wisdom of daily life, wrung from the lips of men forced to learn by hardness and defeat and loss; and then the words that Alfred had first sung were as those of one who knew more than Odin, and yet spoke of daily troubles and the wisdom that grows thereout. But now the things that he sang must needs have come from wisdom beyond that of men--wisdom beyond thought of mine. And if so it seemed to me, I know not how the heart of the scald, who was more thoughtful and knew more than I, was stirred.

He rose up when Alfred ceased, and walked away down the hillside slowly, as in a dream, not looking at us; and the kindly Saxons smiled gently, and said nothing to rouse him.

It is in my mind that Harek's eyes were wet, for he had lost somewhat--his belief in things he held dearest and first of all--and had as yet found nothing that should take its place. There is nought harder than that to a man.

When he had passed out of hearing, I said:

"Are there wiser things yet that you may sing?"

"Ay, and that you may learn, my son," answered Neot. "Listen."

Then he spoke words from Holy Writ that I know now--the words that speak of where wisdom may be found. And he said thereafter, and truly, that it was not all.

Then I seemed to fear greatly.

"Not now, my king, not now," I said; "it is enough."

Then those two spoke to me out of their kind hearts. Yet to me the old gods were very dear, and I clung to them. Neither Neot nor the king said aught against them, being very wise, at that time.

Presently Harek came back, and his eyes were shining.

"Tell me more of this learning," he said, casting himself down on the grass at Alfred's feet. "Scald have I been since I could sing, and nought have I heard like this."

"Some day," Neot said; "it is enough now that you should know what you have heard."

So ended that strange song strife on Neot's quiet hillside. The sun set, and the fleecy mists came up from the little river below, and we sat silent till Alfred rose and said farewell, and we went to the guest house in the village.

Now I think that none will wonder that after we had been with Neot for those ten days, we were ready and willing to take on us the "prime signing," as they called it, gladly and honestly. So we were signed with the cross by Neot, and Alfred and Ethelnoth and Guerir were our witnesses.

I know that many scoff at this, because there are heathen who take this on them for gain, that they may trade more openly, or find profit among Christian folk, never meaning or caring to seek further into the faith that lies open, as it were, before them. But it was not so with us, nor with many others. We were free to serve our old gods if we would, but free also to learn the new faith; and to learn more of it for its own sake seemed good to us.

So we went back to Exeter with the king, and Neot came for a few miles with us, on foot as was his wont, parting from us with many good words. And after he was gone the king was cheerful, and spoke with me about the ordering of the fleet we were to build, as though he were certain that I should take command of it in the spring.

And, indeed, after that time there was never any question among us three vikings about it. It seemed to us that if we had lost Norway as a home, we had gained what would make as good a country; and, moreover, Alfred won us to him in such wise that it seemed we could do nought but serve him. There can be few who have such power over men's hearts as he.

Exeter seemed very quiet when we came back; for the Danes were gone, and the king's levies had dispersed, and only the court remained, though that was enough to make all the old city seem very gay to those who had known it only in the quiet of peace.

One man was there whom I had hardly thought to meet again, and that was Osmund the Danish jarl. For he was a hostage in the king's hands, to make more sure that the peace would be kept. I knew there were hostages to be given by the beaten host; but I had not asked who they were, and had been at the ships when they were given up, ten of them in all, and of the best men among the Danes.

Alfred treated his captives very well, giving them good lodgings, and bating them often at his own table, so that I saw much of Osmund. And more than that, I saw much of the Lady Thora, his daughter, who would not leave him. I do not think that there could be more certain manner of beginning a close friendship between a warrior and the lady whom he shall learn to hold first in his heart, than that in which I first met this fair maiden.

Now one will say that straightway I must fall in love with her, but it was not so: first of all, because I had not time, since every day Alfred planned new ships with me and Thord; and next, because I was his guest, and Osmund was his hostage. Maybe I thought not much of that, however, not having the thoughts of a Saxon towards a Dane. But I will say this, that among all the fair ladies of the queen's household there was none of whom I thought at all; while of what Thora would say I thought often, and it pleased me that the Lady Etheldreda, Odda's fair eldest daughter, took pity on the lonely maiden, and made much of her after a time.

Three weeks I was in Exeter, and then the king went eastward through his country to repair what damage had been done. Then I took up my work for him, and got out my ship and sailed westward, putting into every harbour where a ship might be built, and set the shipwrights to work, having with me royal letters to sheriffs and port reeves everywhere that they should do what I ordered them. In each yard I left two or three of my men, that they should oversee all things; because if one Saxon thinks he knows better than his fellow, he will not be ruled by him, whereas no man can dispute what a born viking has to say about ship craft. It seemed that all were glad of our coming, and the work began very cheerfully.

All this took long, but at last I came up the Severn, and so into the river Parret--for the weather would serve me no longer and laid up the ship in a creek there is at Bridgwater, where Heregar, the king's standard bearer, was sheriff. He made me very welcome at his great house near by, at Cannington, and then rode with me to Bristol; and there I set two ships in frame, and so ended all I could do for the winter. King Alfred would have a fleet when the spring came.

Then Heregar and I would go to Chippenham, to spend the time of the Yule feast with King Alfred; and we rode there with Harek and Kolgrim, and were made most welcome. Many friends whom I had made at Exeter were there, and among them, quiet and yet hopeful of release, were the hostages.

That was a wonderful Yule to me; but I will say little of it, for the tale of the most terrible Twelfth Night that England has ever known overshadows it all, though there were things that I learned at that time, sitting in the church with Harek, at the west end, and listening, that are bright to me. But they are things by themselves, and apart from all else.

Now peace was on all the land, and the frost and snow were bright and sharp everywhere; so that men said that it was a hard winter, and complained of the cold which seemed nothing to us Northmen. Maybe there was a foot of snow in deep places, and the ice was six inches thick on the waters; and the Saxons wondered thereat, saying that they minded the like in such and such years before. Then I would tell them tales of the cold north to warm them, but I think they hardly believed me.

The town was full of thanes and their families who had been called to Alfred's Yule keeping, and it was very bright and pleasant among them all, though here and there burnt ruins made gaps between the houses, minding one that the Danes had held the place not so long since.

So they kept high feasting for Yule and the New Year, and the last great feast was for Twelfth Night, and all were bidden for that, and there was much pleasant talk of what revels should be in the evening.

The day broke very bright and fair, with a keen, windless frost that made the snow crisp and pleasant to ride over, hindering one in no way. And there was the sun shining over all in a way that made the cold seem nought to me, so that I had known nothing more pleasant than this English winter, having seen as yet nothing of the wet and cold times that come more often than such as this. Then, too, the clear ringing of the bells from every village near and far was new to me, and I thought I had heard nothing sweeter than the English call to the church for high festival [lxi].

So I went to the king, and asked him if I might take with me the Danish jarl for a ride beyond the town; for the hostages were only free inside the walls, and I knew this would please Osmund and Thora well. I said that I would see to his safety and be answerable for him.

"This must be Osmund, I suppose," the king said, smiling. "I have heard how you came to know him and his fair daughter at Wareham. It was well done, though maybe I should blame you for running over-much risk."

"I think I ran little, lord king," I said; "and I could have done no less for the poor maiden."

"Surely; but I meant that to go at all was over dangerous."

"I am ready to do the same again for you, my king," I said. "And after all I was in no danger."

Then said the king, smiling gravely at me:

"Greater often are the dangers one sees not than those which one has to meet. I have my own thoughts of what risk you ran."

"Well, take your fair lady and the jarl also where you will. But the feast is set for two hours after noon, and all must be there."

So I thanked him, and he bade me ask his steward for horses if I would, and I went straight to Osmund from his presence.

"I think it will be a more pleasant ride than our last," said Thora. "Yet that is one that I shall not forget."

Then I tried to say that I hoped she did not regret it either, but I minded me of the loved nurse she had to leave, and was silent in time. Yet I thought that she meant nothing of sorrow in the remembrance as she spoke.

We called out my two comrades, for Osmund liked them well, and rode away northward, that the keen air might be behind us as we returned. That was all the chance that led us that way, and it was well that we were so led, as things turned out.

The white downs and woodlands sparkling with frost were very beautiful as we rode, and we went fast and joyously in the fresh air; but the countryside was almost deserted, for the farmsteads were burned when the Danes broke in on the land last spring, and few were built up as yet. The poor folk were in the town now, for the most part, finding empty houses enough to shelter them, and none left to whom they belonged.

Now we rode for twelve miles or so, and then won to a hilltop which we had set as our turning place. I longed to stand there and look out over all this country, that seemed so fair after the rugged northern lands I had known all my life. But when we were there we saw a farmstead just below us, on the far slope of the gentle hill; and we thought it well to go there and dismount, and maybe find some food for ourselves and the horses before turning back.

So we went on. It was but a couple of furlongs distant, and the buildings lay to the right of the road, up a tree-shaded lane of their own.

We turned into this, and before we had gone ten yards along it I halted suddenly. I had seen somewhat that seemed strange, and unmeet for the lady to set eyes on.

"Bide here, jarl," I said, "and let us go on and see what is here; the place looks deserted."

And I looked meaningly at him, glancing at Thora.

But he had seen what had caught my eye, and he stayed at once, turning back into the main road, and beckoning Harek to come with him and Thora, for some reason of his own.

Then Kolgrim and I went on. What we had seen was a man lying motionless by the farm gate, in a way that was plain enough to me. And when we came near, we knew that the man had been slain. He was a farm thrall, and he had a pitchfork in his hand, the shaft of which was half cut through, as with a sword stroke that he had warded from him, though he had not stayed a second cut, for so he was killed.

"Here is somewhat strangely wrong," I said.

"Outlaws' work," answered Kolgrim; for the wartime had made the masterless folk very bold everywhere, and the farm was lonely enough.

We rode through the swinging gate, and then we saw three horses by the stable yard paling, and with them was an armed man, who saw us as we came round the house, and whistled shrilly. Whereon two others came running from the building, and asked in the Danish tongue what he called for. The first man pointed to us, and all three mounted at once. They were in mail and helm, fully armed.

Now we were not, for we had thought of no meeting such as this, and rode in woollen jerkins and the like, and had only our swords and seaxes, as usual; but for the moment I did not think that we should need either. Outlaws such as I took them for do not make any stand unless forced.

Presently one of the men, having mounted leisurely enough, called to us.

"There is no plunder to be had," he said, "even if you were not too late; our folk cleared out the place over well last time."

Then a fourth man, one who seemed of some rank, rode from beyond the house, passing behind us without paying any heed to us, except that he called to the men to follow him, and so went down the lane towards where Osmund was waiting with Harek.

All this puzzled me, and so I cried to the three men:

"What do you here? Whose men are you?"

At that they looked at one another--they were not more than ten yards from us now--and halted.

"You should know that," one said; and then he put his hand to his sword suddenly, adding in a sharp voice:

"These be Saxons; cut them down."

When hand goes to sword hilt one knows what is coming, and even as the man said his last words I was on them, and Kolgrim was not a pace behind me. The Dane's sword was out first; but I was upon him in time. His horse swerved as mine plunged forward, and I rode him down, horse and man rolling together in the roadway. Then the man to my right cut at me, and I parried the blow and returned it. Then that horse was riderless, and I heard Kolgrim laugh as his man went down with a clatter and howl.

My horse plunged on for a few steps, and then I turned. Kolgrim had one horse by the bridle, and was catching that which had fallen. I caught the other, and so we looked at each other.

"This is your luck, master," said Kolgrim.

"Well," said I, "these are Danes, and I do not think they are wanderers either. Here are forage bags behind the saddles. One would say that they were on the march if this were not mid-winter and time of peace. The horsemen in advance of a host, or the like."

Then Kolgrim said:

"Where has the other man gone? I had forgotten him for the moment."

"Bide here and see if any poor farm folk are yet alive," I said. "I will ride after him."

So I gave the horse I was holding to my comrade, and went back quickly down the lane to where Osmund and the other two were. The man I sought was speaking with the jarl, whose face was white and troubled. Harek was looking red and angry, but on Thora's face was written what I could not understand--as it were some fear of a new terror.

Now it was plain that all three were very glad of my coming; but the stranger looked round for a single glance, and then went on speaking to Osmund.

"Be not a fool, jarl," he said angrily. "Here is your chance; let it not slip."

"I tell you that my word shall not be broken," Osmund replied, very coldly and sternly.

"What say you, girl?" the man said then, turning to Thora. "Short shrift will be the jarl's when Alfred finds that we are on him."

But Thora turned away without a word, and then the Dane spoke to me:

"Here! you are another hostage, I suppose."

"I am not," I answered.

"Well, then, here is Jarl Osmund, if you know him not, and he is one. Tell him that what I say is true, and that Chippenham town will be burned out tonight king and all."

I saw that the Dane, seeing that I was armed, and not clad in the Saxon manner altogether, took me for one of his own people. And from his words it was plain that some of the Danish chiefs had broken away from Guthrum, and were making this unheard-of mid-winter march to surprise Alfred. Most likely they were newcomers into Mercia, and had nought to do with the Exeter host.

"Maybe it is true," I answered; "but I am no Dane."

He laughed loudly.

"Why, then, you are one of Alfred's Norsemen! Now I warn you to get away from Chippenham, for it is unsafe, and there will be no king to pay you tomorrow. I think that you will say with me that it were better for Osmund to come with me to meet the host than to go back to Alfred and be hung before he flies--if he gets news of us in time to do so."

Herein the man was right, for Alfred had warned the chiefs at Exeter that he held the hostages in surety for peace on the part of all and any Danes. But I thought I might learn more, so I said:

"Guthrum thinks little of his friends' lives."

"Guthrum!" the Dane answered sneeringly; "what have we to do with him and his peace making?"

"What then are you Hubba's men?"

"He is in Wales. Think you that we are all tied to the sons of Lodbrok?"

"You might have worse leaders," I said.

And just then Kolgrim came along the lane, leading the three horses, and on them were the armour and weapons of the slain. It was not my comrade's way to leave for other folk aught that was worth having.

At once the Dane knew what had happened, and he swung his horse round and spurred it fiercely, making for flight. Then Harek looked at me and touched his sword hilt, and I nodded. It was well to let no tidings of our knowledge go back to the host. After the Dane therefore went Harek, and I looked at Osmund.

"Jarl," I said, "I am in a strait here. If you go back, your life is in Alfred's hands."

"I know it," he said, smiling faintly. "It is a hard place maybe for us both, but there is only one way. You must get back to the king, and I with you; for you have to answer for me, and my word is passed not to escape."

Then Thora said:

"The king is just, as all men know. How should he slay you for what you cannot help?"

"Ay," he answered, smiling at her, "that is right."

So she was satisfied, knowing nought perhaps of what the place of a hostage is.

So we started back to Chippenham quickly, and after us I heard Harek coming. He had a led horse when he joined us, and I knew that none would take word to the Danish host that the king was warned.

When we came to the hilltop over which we had ridden so blithely an hour ago or less, we looked back, and at first saw nothing. Then over the white brow of a rolling down that shone in the level sunlight came a black speck that grew and lengthened, sliding, as it were, like a snake down the hillside. And that line sparkled like ice in the sunlight from end to end; for it was the Danish host on the march, and in two hours they would be where we stood, and in two more they who were mounted would be in Chippenham streets, where Alfred had not enough men even to guard the gates against such a force as was coming.

Then we rode hard for the lives of all who were in the town, and as I went I thought also that we rode to the death of the brave, honest jarl who was beside me, saying nothing, but never letting his horse falter. Just as bravely rode Thora.

In an hour we were at the gates, and I rode straight to the king's house, and sought him on urgent business.

Ethered of Mercia came out to me.

"What is it, Ranald?" he said. "The Witan is set now."

I told him in few words, and his face changed.

"It seems impossible in frost and snow," he said.

"Ay; but there are proofs," I said, pointing through the great doorway.

There was my party, and Kolgrim was binding a wound on Harek's arm of which I knew nought till that moment, and the led horses and spoils were plain enough to say all.

Then Ethered made haste and took me to the great hall, where Alfred sat with some thirty thanes of his Witan [lxii], and many clergy. I knew they were to meet on some business that I had nought to do with. Ethered went to the king without any ceremony, and speaking low told him my message. Whereon the king's face grew white and then red, and he flashed out into terrible wrath:

"Forsworn and treacherous!" he cried, in a thick voice that shook with passion. "The hostages--chain them and bring them here. Their friends shall find somewhat waiting them here that shall make them wish they had kept their oaths!"

Then he said to me:

"Speak out, Ranald, and tell these thanes your news."

I spoke plainly, and they listened with whitening faces and muttered oaths. And when I ceased, one cried, hardly knowing what he said, as I think:

"This outlander rode with Osmund the Dane to bring them on us even now."

"Silence!" Alfred said; and then in a cold voice he asked me:

"Where is this Osmund? I suppose he has fled to his people."

"That he has not, though he could have done so," I answered. "Moreover, the Dane I spoke with said in so many words that this is no host of Guthrum's."

At that Alfred frowned fiercely.

"Whose then? What good is a king if he cannot make his people keep their oaths?"

There was a stir at the door, and the eyes of all turned that way. And when the thanes saw that the hostages were being led in, with Osmund at their head, a great sullen growl of wrath broke from them, and I thought all hope was gone for the lives of those captives.

"Hear you this?" the king said, in a terrible voice, when the noise ceased. "By the deed of your own people your lives are forfeit. They have broken the peace, and even now are marching on us. Your leader, Osmund himself, has seen them."

"It is true," Osmund said. "We are in the king's hands."

Then Alfred turned to the Witan, who were in disorder, and in haste, as one might see, to be gone to their houses and fly.

"You heard the Danish oath taken at Exeter; what is your word on this?"

They answered in one voice:

"Slay them. What else?"

"You hear," said the king to the Danes. "Is not the sentence just?"

"It is what one might look for," Osmund answered, "but I will say this, that this is some new band of Danes, with whom we have nought to do."

"What!" said Alfred coldly; "will you tell me that any Dane in the country did not know that I held hostages for the peace? Go to.

"See to this matter, sheriff."

Then the sheriff of Chippenham came forward, and it seemed to me that it was of no use for me to say aught; yet I would try what I could do, so I spoke loudly, for a talk had risen among the thanes.

"What is this, lord king? Will you slay Osmund the jarl, who has kept his troth, even to coming back to what he knew would be his death? You cannot slay such a man for the oath breaking of others."

Then the king looked long at me, and the sheriff stayed, and at first I expected passionate words; but the king's rage was cold and dreadful now.

"His friends slay him--not I," he answered.

Then of a sudden I minded somewhat, and clear before me stood a test by which I might know certainly if it were good that I should leave the Asir and follow the way of the white Christ.

"King Alfred," I said, "I have heard the bishop tell, in the great church here, of a king who slew the guiltless at Christmastide. There was nought too hard for any to say of that man. Moreover, I have heard strange and sweet words of peace at this time, of forgiveness of enemies and of letting go of vengeance. Are these things nought, or are they indeed those by which you guide yourselves, as Neot says?"

He was silent, gazing fixedly on me; and all the Witan were speechless, listening.

"These men are enemies maybe, but they at least have done nought. Shall you avenge yourself on them for the wrongdoing of others?"

Then the king's face changed, and he looked past me, and in his eyes grew and shone a wondrous light, and slowly he lifted up his hand, and cried, in a great voice that seemed full of joy:

"Hear this, O ye Danes and foes of the Cross. For the love of Christ, and in His name, I bid you go in peace!"

And then, as they stared at him in wonder and awe at his look and words, Alfred said to me:

"Unbind them, my brother, and let them go--nay, see them safely to some strong house; for the poor folk may slay them in their blind anger, even as would I have done."

Then no man hindered me--for it seemed as if a great fear, as of the might of the holy name, had fallen on all--and I went and cut the bonds of the captives. And as I did so, Osmund said in a low voice to me:

"First daughter and then father. We owe our lives to you."

"Nay," I answered, "but to the Christians' faith."

Then I hurried them out before news of what was on hand could get among the townsfolk, and we went quickly to my lodgings; for that was a strong house enough, and could be barred in such wise that even if any tried to attack the place in the flight that would begin directly, it would take too long to break the doors down to be safe with the host at hand.

Then came Heregar, armed and mounted, with a single man behind him, and he called for me.

"Ride out with me, King Ranald, for we must count these Danes, and see that we are not overrating their number. After that we will join the king, who goes to Glastonbury."

So I bade farewell to Osmund and to Thora, who said nought, but looked very wistfully, as if she would say words of thanks but could not; and at that I went quickly, for it seemed hard to leave her, in some way that was not clear to me, amid all the turmoil of the place.

But when we were on the road, Heregar said to me:

"It is in my mind that Osmund, your friend, will fare ill among these Danes. They will hear how he rode back, and will hold that by his means the king escaped."

"What can be done?"

"The man is one of a thousand, as it seems to me. Let us bid him leave the town and get back to Guthrum as he can."

"He can have the Danish horses," I said.

Now before sunset we had seen the Danish force, and our hearts sank. There were full ten thousand men, many of whom were mounted.

Then we rode back, and found the town in such tumult as it is not good to think on. There is nothing more terrible to see than such a flight, and in midwinter.

When we came to my lodging, Heregar went in to find Osmund. I would not see him again, lest Thora should weep. But in a few minutes he came out with the jarl.

"Here is a wise man," said Heregar. "He says that he swore to keep the peace with Alfred, and he will do it. He and the Lady Thora will go with us. There are one or two also of the other hostages who blame him for returning. He cannot stay among the Danes here."

Then I was very glad, and we made haste to have all ready for Thora's comfort on the ride that might be so long. And so we rode out after the king along the road to Glastonbury, and I think that the Danes were in the town half an hour after we left it.

Next we knew that Danes were on the road before us, and that more were hard after us. Some had skirted the town in order to cut off the king, and were pursuing him. So we struck off the road into by-lanes that Heregar knew, resting at lonely houses as we went on. And when we came to Glastonbury at last, the king was not there, nor did any know of his fate.

Then we rode, with the Danes swarming everywhere, through the Sedgemoor wastes to Bridgwater, and found rest at Cannington, Heregar's great house not far off.

Chapter IX. The Sign of St. Cuthberht.

I suppose that in our flight from Glastonbury to Bridgwater we passed through more dangers than we knew of; for Danes were hard after us, riding even into sight from the town that evening, and next day coming even to the eastern end of the old bridge, and bandying words with the townsfolk who guarded it. Across it they dared not come, for there is a strong earthwork on the little rise from the river, which guards both bridge and town, and in it were my Norsemen with the townsfolk.

So we were in safety for a time; and it seemed likely that we might be so for long if but a few men could be gathered, for here was a stretch of country that was, as it were, a natural fastness. Three hundred years ago the defeated Welsh had turned to bay here while Kenwalch of Wessex and his men could not follow them; and now it seemed likely that here in turn would Wessex stand her ground.

It is a great square-sided patch of rolling, forest-covered country, maybe twelve miles long from north to south, and half as much across. None can enter it from the north, because there is the sea, and a wild coast that is not safe for a landing; on the west the great, steep, fort-crested Quantock Hills keep the border; on the eastern side is the river Parret, and on the north the Tone, which joins it. Except at Bridgwater, at the eastern inland corner, and Taunton, at the western--one at the head of the tidal waters of the Parret, and the other guarding the place where the Quantocks end--there is no crossing the great and wide-stretching fens of Sedgemoor and Stanmoor and the rest that lie on either bank of the rivers. Paths there are that the fenmen know, winding through mere and peat bog and swamp, but no host can win through them; and perhaps those marches are safer borders than even the sea.

If one came from the sea, one must land at Watchet, and then win a path across the Quantocks, and there is the ancient camp of Dowsborough to block the way; or else put into the Parret, and there, at the first landing place, where they say that Joseph of Arimathaea landed, bearing the holy thorn staff in his hand, is the strong hill fort of Combwich, old as the days of that Joseph, or maybe older.

So with walled towns and hill forts the corners of Heregar's land were kept; and with sea and marsh and hill the sides were strong, and we thought to find Alfred the king here before us. But he was not; and next day we rode on to Taunton to seek him there, for that was the strongest fortress in that part of the west. And again he was not to be heard of. Then fear for his life began to creep into our minds, and we came back to Cannington sorely downcast.

Then Heregar spoke to me very kindly of what he thought I could best do, and it was nothing more or less than that I should leave this land, which seemed to have no hope of honour for me now.

"Go rather to Rolf, your countryman," he said. "There is great talk of his doings in Neustria [lxiii] beyond the Channel. It is your kindness only that holds you here, King Ranald, and there wait glory and wealth for you and your men."

So he urged me for a little while, not giving me time to answer him as I would; but when I said nothing he stayed his words, and then I spoke plainly, and it was good to see his face light up as I did so.

"It shall not be said of me that I left King Alfred, who has been my good friend, in time of trouble; rather will I stay here and do what I can to help him out of it. Why, there are ships that I have put in frame for him in the western ports that the Danes will not reach yet, if at all. When spring comes we will man them and make a landing somewhere, and so divide the Danish host at least."

"Now I will say no more," answered the thane, putting his hand on mine. "Speak thus to the king when we find him, and it will do him good, for I think that when he left Chippenham he was well-nigh despairing."

"It is hard to think that of Alfred," I said.

"Ay; but I saw his face as he rode away just before I sought you. Never saw I such a look on a man's face before, and I pray that I may not see it again. It was terrible to look on him, for I think he had lost all hope."

"For the time, maybe," I said; "but I cannot believe that when the first weight of the blow passed he was not himself again."

Presently there came a shift of wind and a quick thaw with driving rain, and floods grew and spread rapidly in the low-lying lands. One good thing can be said of this weather, and that was that because of it the Danes burned neither town nor farmstead, needing all the shelter they could find.

Three days that gale lasted, and then the wind flew round again to the north, with return of the frost in even greater strength than before; and the weather-wise fishers and shepherds said that this betokened long continuance thereof, and so it seemed likely to be.

But through it all we heard no tidings of the king; and in one way that was good, for had he been taken by the Danes, they would have let all men know thereof soon enough. But we feared that he might have been slain by some party who knew not who he was, and that fear hung heavily over us all.

Next we had a messenger from Odda, who was at Exeter, asking for sure word of what had befallen; and the one hope we had yet was gone, for he too knew nothing.

Very sad and silent was Osmund the jarl, though he and Thora were most kindly received as honoured guests by the Lady Alswythe and the household of the thane.

Once I asked him what his plans were, for we were both strangers, and I knew him best.

"Presently," he said, "I shall try to get back to Guthrum. While I am here I will be held as if I were no one--as a harmless ghost who walks the house, neither seeing nor hearing aught. If there were Welsh to be fought, I would fight beside you all, gladly, for Alfred; but as the war is against my own folk, I can do nothing. I will neither fight for them nor fight against them; for King Alfred and you, my friend, gave me life, and it is yours. I think that some day I may be of use to Alfred in helping to bring about a lasting peace."

"If we find him," I said.

"Ay, you will find him. He is hiding now for some wise reason that we shall know. I think it is not known how his plans are feared by our folk. I am sure that of this midwinter march the Danes will say that it is worthy of Alfred himself."

Nevertheless we heard nothing of him, though the thane had men out everywhere trying to gain news. All that they heard was the same tale of dismay from whoever they might meet, and I think that but for a chance we should not have found him until he chose to come forth from his refuge.

Heregar the thane had a strange serving man, the same who had ridden with him and me to meet the Danish forces; and this man was a fenman from Sedgemoor, who knew all the paths through the wastes. Lean and loose-limbed he was, and somewhat wild looking, mostly silent; but where his lord went he went also. They said that he had saved the thane's life more than once in the great battles about Reading, when the Danish host first came.

This man was out daily, seeking news with the rest; and one day, just a week after we had come to Cannington, when the frost had bound everything fast again, he came home and sought his master.

Heregar and I and Osmund sat together silently before the fire, and he looked from one to the other of us outlanders.

"Speak out, Dudda," said Heregar, who knew his ways; "here are none but friends."

"Ay, friends of ours sure enough; but are they the king's?"

"Most truly so. Have you news of him?"

"I have not; but I have heard some fenmen talking."

Then Osmund rose up and went his way silently, as was his wont; and Dudda grinned at us.

"He is a good Dane," he said; "now I can speak. They say there is some great lord hiding in the fens beyond the round hill where Tone and Parret join, that we call the Stane--somewhere by Long Hill, they say. Now I mind that one day when the king rode with you across the Petherton heights, he looked out over all the fens, and called me and asked much of them. And when I told him what he would, he said, 'Here is a place where a man might lie hid from all the world if he chose.' So he laughed, and we rode on."

"I mind it," said Heregar; "but it was many years ago."

"I think he may be there, for our king weighs his words, and does not forget. I held his horse at your door in Chippenham the other day, and he spoke to me by name, and put me in mind of little things for which he had laughed at me in those same old days. He is a good king."

So said Dudda, the rough housecarl; and it is in my mind that the kindly remembrance would have wiped out many a thought of wrong, had there been any. That is a kingly gift to remember all, and no king has ever been great who has not had it; for it binds every man to his prince when he knows that aught he has done is not forgotten, so it be good to recall.

So it came to pass that next day, very early, we rode away, taking Harek and Kolgrim and this man Dudda with us, well armed and mounted and full of hope, across the southward ridge that looks down over the fens of the meeting of Tone and Parret, where they are widest and wildest. No Danes had crossed them yet, and when I saw what they were like I thought that they never could do so.

And as I looked at the long chains of ice-bound meres and pools that ran among dense thickets of alder and wide snow-covered stretches of peat bogs, it seemed that we might search in vain for one who would hide among them. Only the strange round hill on Stanmoor seemed to be a point that might be noted on all the level, though Dudda told us that there were many islets hidden in the wooded parts.

We went to the lower hills and then to the very edge of the fenland, skirting along it, and asking here and there of the cottagers if they knew of any folk in hiding in the islets. But though we heard of poor people in one or two places, none of them knew of any thane; and the day wore on, and hope began to grow dim, save for Dudda's certainty that what he had heard was true.

At last we came to a long spur of high ground that runs out into the fen, about midway between Bridgwater and Taunton; and there is the village they call Lyng, where we most hoped to hear good news. The day was drawing to sunset, and we would hasten; so Heregar went one way and I another, each to distant cottages that we saw. The lane down which I and my two comrades rode seemed to lead fenwards, and it was little more than a track, deep in snow and tree bordered. The cottage we sought was a quarter mile away when we left the thane, and as we drew near it we saw an old woman walking away from it, and from us also. She did not seem to hear us when we called to her; and, indeed, such was the fear of Danes that often folk would fly when they saw us, and the faster because we called, not waiting to find out who we were.

Then from out of the cottage came another old woman, who hobbled into the track and looked after the first, shaking her fist after her, and then following her slowly, looking on the ground. She never glanced our way at all, and our horses made no noise to speak of in the snow.

We drew up to her, and then I saw that she had a hammer in her right hand and a broad-headed nail in her left. I wondered idly what she was about with these things, when she stooped and began to hammer the nail into the iron-hard ground, and I could hear her muttering some words quickly.

I reined up to watch her, puzzled, and said to Harek:

"Here is wizardry; or else what is the old dame about?"

"It is somewhat new to me," the scald said, looking on with much interest; for if he could learn a new spell or charm, he was pleased as if he had found a treasure.

Then I saw that she was driving the nail into a footprint. There were three tracks only along the snow--two going away from the cottage and one returning. That which went and returned was made by this old woman, as one might see from her last steps, which made a fourth track from the door.

"She is hammering the nail into her own footprint," I said, noting this.

Now she sang in a cracked voice, hammering savagely the while; and now and then she shook her fist or hammer, or both, towards where the other old dame had gone out of sight round a bend of the lane.

Then she put her hand to her back and straightened herself with a sort of groan, as old dames will, and slowly turned round and saw us.

Whereat she screamed, and hurled the hammer at Kolgrim, who was laughing at her, cursing us valiantly for Danes and thieves, and nearly hitting him.

"Peace, good mother," I said; "we are not Danes. Here is earnest thereof," and I threw her a sceatta from my pouch.

She clutched it from the ice pool where it fell, and stared at us, muttering yet. Then Harek spoke to her.

"Mother, I have much skill in spells, but I know not what is wrought with hammer and nail and footprint. I would fain learn."

"Little know you of spells if you know not that," she said, having lost all fear of us, as it seemed.

"I am only a northerner," Harek said. "Maybe 'tis a spell against a sprained ankle, which seems likely. I only know one for that."

"Which know you?" she said scornfully; "you are over young to meddle with such like."

"This," said Harek. "It works well if the sprain be bathed with spring-cold water, while one says it twice daily:

```
"'Baldur and Woden
Went to the woodland;
There Baldur's foal fell,
Wrenching its foot.'
```

"That is how it begins."

Then the old woman's eyes sparkled.

"Ay; that is good. Learn it me, I pray you. Now I know that you have wizardry, for you name the old gods."

"Tell me first what hammer and nail work in footprint."

"Why, yon old hag has overlooked me," she said savagely. "Now, if one does as I have done, one nails her witchcraft to herself [xiii]."

"Whose footprint does the nail go into?" Harek asked.

"Why, hers surely. Now this is the spell," and she chanted somewhat in broad Wessex, and save that Baldur's name and Thor's hammer also came into it, I do not know what it all was. I waxed impatient now, for I thought that Heregar might be waiting for us.

But she and Harek exchanged spells, and then I said:

"Now, dame, know you of any thane in hiding hereabouts?"

Thereat she looked sharply at me.

"I know nothing. Here be I, lamed, in the cottage all day."

"There is a close friend of mine in hiding from the Danes somewhere here," I said, doubting, from her manner, if she spoke the truth. "I would take him to a safer place."

"None safer," she answered. "What is his name?"

Then I doubted for a moment; but Harek's quick wit helped me.

"Godred," he said; for the name by which the king had called himself once it was likely that he would use again.

"I know of no thanes," she said, though not at once, so that I was sure she knew somewhat more than she thought safe to tell.

Then she was going, but Harek stayed her.

"Yours is a good spell against the evil eye, mother," he said, "but I can tell you a better."

"What is it?" she said eagerly.

"News for news," he answered carelessly. "Tell us if you know aught of this thane, and I will tell you."

"I said not that there was a thane." she said at once.

"Nay, mother; but you denied it not. Come now; I think what I can tell you will save you trouble."

She thought for a little, weighing somewhat in her mind, as it seemed, and then she chose to add to her store of witchcraft.

"Yonder, then," she said, nodding to the dense alder thickets that hid the river Tone from us, across a stretch of frozen mere or flooded land. "I wot well that he who bides in Denewulf's cottage is a thane, for he wears a gold ring, and wipes his hands in the middle of the towel, and sits all day studying and troubling in his mind in such wise that he is no good to any one--not even turning a loaf that burns on the hearth before his eyes. Ay, they call him Godred."

Then my heart leaped up with gladness, and I turned to seek Heregar; but he was coming, and so I waited. Then the dame clamoured for her reward, which Harek had as nearly forgotten as had I.

"Mother," the scald said gravely, "when I work a spell with hammer and nail, the footprint into which the nail is driven is of her who cast the evil eye on me."

"Why, so it should be."

"Nay, but you drive it into your own," he said.

She looked, and then looked again. Then she stamped a new print alongside the nailed one, and it was true. She had paid no heed to the matter in her fury, and when she knew that she turned pale.

"Man," she cried, "help me out of this. I fear that I have even nailed the evil overlooking fast to myself."

"Ay, so you have," said Harek; "but it is you who know little of spells if you cannot tell what to do. Draw the nail out while saying the spell backwards, and then put it into the right place carefully. Then you will surely draw away also any ill that she has already sent you, and fasten it to her."

"Then I think she will shrivel up," said the old witch, with much content. "You are a great wizard, lord; and I thank you."

"Here is a true saying of a friend of mine," said Heregar, coming up in time to hear this. "But what has come to you, king? have you heard aught?"

Now when the old woman heard the thane name the king, before I could answer she cried out and came and clung to my stirrup, taking my hand and kissing it, and weeping over it till I was ashamed.

"What is this?" I said.

"O my lord the king!" she cried. "I thought that yon sad-faced man in Denewulf's house was our king maybe, so wondrous proud are his ways, and so strange things they hear him speak when he sleeps. But now I am glad, for I have seen the king and kissed his hand, and, lo, the sight of him is good. Ay, but glad will all the countryside be to know that you live."

Then I knew not what to say; but Heregar beckoned to me, saying:

"Come, leave her her joy; it were cruel to spoil it, and maybe she will never know her mistake."

So we rode on, and Heregar called Dudda, asking him if he knew Denewulf's cottage; while in the track stood the witch, blessing her king as eagerly as she had cursed her gossip just now.

"I know not the path, though I have heard of the cottage," Dudda said; "but it will be strange if I cannot find a way to the place."

He took us carefully into the fen for some way until we passed through a thicket and came to the edge of a mere, and there were five men who bore fishing nets and eel spears, which had not been used, as one might suppose, seeing that the ice was nigh a foot thick after the thaw and heavy frost again.

And those two men who came first were Ethelnoth, the Somerset ealdorman, and young Ethered of Mercia. It was strange to see those nobles bearing such burdens; but we knew that we had found the king.

They saw us, and halted; but Heregar waved his hand, and they came on, for they knew him. It would be hard to say which party was the more pleased to meet the other.

"Where is the king?" we asked.

"Come with us, and we will take you to him," Ethered said. "But supperless you must be tonight. We have nought in the house, and nothing can we catch."

Then I was surprised, and said:

"Is it so bad as that here? In our land, when the ice is at its thickest we can take as much fish as we will easily."

"Save us from starvation, Ranald," said Ethered, laughing ruefully, "and we will raise a big stone heap here in your honour."

"Kolgrim will show you," I said; "let me go to the king."

"I am a great ice fisherman," said Harek; "let me go also."

Then Heregar laughed in lightness of heart.

"Ay, wizard, go also. There will be charms of some sort needed before Ethered sees so much as a scale."

Whereon they dismounted, and Kolgrim took his axe from his saddle bow, asking where the river was, while he wondered that such a simple matter as breaking a hole in the ice and dropping a line among the hungry fish, who would swarm to the air, had not been thought of. We had not yet learned that such a winter as this comes but seldom to the west of England, and the thanes knew nothing of our northern ways.

Then Ethelnoth led Heregar and me across twisting and almost unseen paths, safer now because of the frost, though one knew that in some places a step to right or left would plunge him through the crust of hard snow into a bottomless peat bog. The alder thickets grew everywhere round dark, ice-bound pools of peat-stained water, and we could nowhere see more than a few yards before us; and it was hard to say how far we had gone from the upland edge of the swamp when the ground began to rise from the fen, and grew harder among better timber. But for the great frost, one would have needed a boat in many places.

Then we came to a clearing, in which stood a house that was hardly more than a cottage, and round it were huts and cattle sheds. And this was where the king was--the house of Denewulf the herdsman, the king's own thrall. There was a rough-wattled stockade round the place, and quick-set fences within which to pen the cattle and swine outside that, and all around were the thickets. None could have known that such an island was here, for not even the house overtopped the low trees; and though all the higher ground was cleared, there were barely two acres above the watery level--a long, narrow patch of land that lay southeast and northwest, with its southerly end close to the banks of the river Tone. Men call the place Athelney now, since the king and his nobles lay there. It had no name until he came, but I think that it will bear ever hereafter that which it earned thus.

Two shaggy grey sheepdogs came out to meet us, changing their angry bark for welcome when they saw Ethelnoth; and a man came to the door to see what roused them, and he had a hunting spear in his hand. I took him for some thane, as he spoke to us in courtly wise; but he was only Denewulf the herdsman himself.

"How fares the king?" asked Ethelnoth.

"His dark hour came on him after you went," Denewulf answered; "and then the pain passed, and he slept well, and now has just wakened wonderfully cheerful. I have not seen him so bright since he came here; and he is looking eagerly for your return, seeming to expect some news."

"It may be that our coming has been foretold him beforehand," said Heregar. "Our king has warnings given him in his dreams at times."

Then from out of the house Alfred's voice hailed us:

"Surely that is the voice of my standard bearer.

"Come in quickly, Heregar, for all men know that hope comes with you."

We went in; and it was a poor place enough for a king's lodging, though it was warm and neat. Alfred sat over the fire in the middle of the larger room of the two which the house had, and a strew of chips and shreds of feathers and the like was round him; for he was arrow making--an art in which he was skilful, and he had all the care and patience which it needs. When we came in he rose up, shaking the litter from his dress into the fire; and we bent our knees to him and kissed his hand.

"O my king," said Heregar, "why have you thus hidden yourself from us? All the land is mourning for you."

Then Alfred looked sadly at him and wistfully, answering:

"First, because I must hide; lastly, because I would be hidden: but between these two reasons is one of which I repent--because I despaired."

"Nay," said Denewulf, "it was not despair; it was grief and anxiousness and thought and waiting for hope. Never have you spoken of despair, my king."

"But I have felt it," he answered, "and I was wrong. Hope should not leave a man while he has life, and friends like these, and counsellors like yourself. Now have I been rebuked, and hope is given me afresh."

Then he smiled and turned to me.

"Why, Ranald my cousin, this is kindness indeed. I had not thought that you would bide with a lost cause, nor should I have thought of blame for you had you gone from this poor England; you are not bound to her as are her sons."

"My king," I said truly, "there are things that bind more closely even than birth."

I think he was pleased, for he smiled, and shook his head at me as though to say that he could not take my saying to himself, as I meant it. And then, before we could ask him more, he began to think of our needs.

"Here we have been pressed for food, friends, for the last few days, and I fear you must fast with us. The deer have fled from our daily hunting, and the wild fowl have sought open water. Unless our fishers have luck, which seems unlikely, we must do as well as we can on oaten bread."

Then Ethelnoth said:

"There have been no fish caught today, my king."

"Why, then, we will wait till the others return; and meanwhile I will hear all the news, for Ranald and Heregar will have much to tell me."

So we told him all that we knew, and he asked many questions, until darkness fell.

"Why are you here, lord king?" asked Heregar; "my hall is safe."

"Your hall and countryside are safe yet because I am not there," Alfred answered, fixing his bright eyes on the thane. "The Danes are hunting for me, and were I in any known place, thither would they come. Therefore I said that now I choose to bide hidden. Moreover, in this quiet and loneliness there comes to me a plan that I think will work out well; for this afternoon, as I slept, I was bidden to look for a sign that out of hopelessness should come help and victory."

Just then the dogs rose up and whined at the door, as if friends came; and there were cheerful voices outside. The door opened, and in stumbled Ethered, bearing a heavy basket of great fish, which he cast on the floor--lean green and golden pike, and red-finned roach, in a glittering, flapping heap.

"Here is supper!" he cried joyfully, "and more than supper, for each of us is thus laden. Fish enough for an army could we have taken had we not held our hands. I could not have thought it possible."

Whereat Alfred rose up and stared, crossing himself.

"*Deo gratias*," he said under his breath, and then said aloud, "Lo, this is the sign of which I spoke even now--that my fishers should return laden with spoil, even for an army, although frost and snow have prevented them from taking fish for many days, and today was less likelihood of their doing so than ever."

"Ranald knew well how this would cheer you, King Alfred," said Ethered, thinking that I had spoken of this as a proof that all was not lost, in some way.

"Ranald said nought; but the sign came from above, thus," the king said gravely. "In my dream the holy Saint Cuthberht stood by my side, and reproved me sharply for my downheartedness and despair, and for my doubt of help against the heathen; and when he knew that I was sorry, he foretold to me that all would yet be well, and that I should obtain the kingdom once more with even greater honour than I have had--with many more wondrous promises. And then he gave me this sign, as I have told you and, behold, it has come, and my heart is full of thankfulness. Now I know that all will be well with England."

Then said Denewulf, who it was plain took no mean place with the king and thanes:

"Say how this miracle was wrought, I pray you, for it is surely such."

"Hither came King Ranald and his two friends and bade us make holes in the ice and fish through them. So we did, and this is what came thereof," said Ethered.

"Therefore King Ranald and his coming are by the hand of God," said Denewulf. "Therein lies the miracle."

Then I was feared, for all were silent in wonder at the coming to pass of the sign; and it seemed to me that I was most truly under a power stronger than that of the old gods, who never wrought the like of this.

Then came Harek's voice outside, where he hung up fish to freeze against the morrow; and he sang softly some old saga of the fishing for the Midgard snake by Asa Thor. And that grated on me, though I ever waited to hear what song the blithe scald had to fit what was on hand, after his custom. Alfred heard too, and he glanced at me, and I was fain to hang my head.

"Ranald, who brought to pass the sign, shall surely share in its bodings of good," he said, quickly and kindly. "I think that he is highly favoured."

Then in came my comrades, and they bent to the king, and he thanked them; and after that was supper and much cheerfulness. Harek sang, and Alfred, and after them Denewulf. Much I marvelled at the wisdom of this strange man, but I never knew how he gained it. King Alfred was ever wont to say that in him he had found his veriest counsellor against despair in that dark time; and when in after days he took him from the fen and made him a bishop, he filled the place well and wisely, being ever the same humble-minded man that I had known in Athelney [xiv].

Chapter X. Athelney and Combwich.

In the morning King Alfred took us to the southern end of his island, and there told us what his plans were. And as we listened they seemed to us to be wiser than mortal mind could have made, so simple and yet so sure were they, as most great plans will be. It is no wonder that his people hold that he was taught them from above.

He bade us look across the fens to the wooded heights of Selwood Forest, to south and east, and to the bold spur of the Polden Hills beyond the Parret that they call Edington. There was nought but fen and river and marsh between them and us--"impassable by the Danes who prowled there. Only at the place where the two rivers join was a steep, rounded hill, that stood up strangely from the level--the hill that they call the Stane, on Stanmoor; and there were other islands like this on which we stood, unseen among the thickets, or so low that one might not know of them until upon them.

"Now," he said, "sooner or later the Danes will know I am here, where they cannot reach me. Therefore I will keep them watching this place until I can strike them a blow that will end the trouble once for all. They will be sure that we gather men on the Quantock side, whence Heregar can keep them; and so, while they watch for us to attack them thence, we will gather beyond Selwood, calling all the thanes from Hants and Wilts and Dorset and Somerset to meet me on a fixed day, and so fall on them. Now we will build a fort yonder on Stane hill that will make them wonder, and so the plan will begin to work. For I have only told you the main lines thereof; the rest must go as can be planned from day to day."

Then he looked steadfastly at the Selwood heights, and added:

"And if the plan fails, and the battle I look for goes against us, there remain Heregar's places yet. Petherton, Combwich, and Dowsborough are good places, where a king may die in a ring of foes, looking out over the land for which his life is given."

"We shall not fail, my king," said Heregar. "Devon will gather to you across the Quantocks also."

"Ay," he said; "and you will need them with you."

Then said I:

"Hubba is in Wales, and is likely to come here when he hears that his fellows are gathering against us. Then will Devon be needed at Combwich in Parret mouth, or at Watchet."

"That will be Devon's work," the king said. "If Hubba comes before your ships are ready to meet him, he must at least be driven to land elsewhere, or our stronghold is taken behind us."

Now I was so sure that Hubba would come, that this seemed to me to be the weakest part of the king's plan. But Alfred thought little of it.

"My stronghold seems to be on Quantock side; it is rather beyond Selwood, in the hearts of my brave thanes and freemen. Fear not, cousin. Hubba will come, and you and Heregar will meet him; and whether you win or not, my plan holds."

Then I knew that the king saw far beyond what was plain to me, and I was very confident in him. And I am sure that I was the only man who had the least doubt from the beginning.

Now, after all was planned, Heregar and I rode back to his place, and sent word everywhere that the king was safe, though he commanded us to tell no man where he lay as yet. None but thanes were to be in the island with him; and from that time the name we knew it by began, as one by one the athelings crossed the fen paths thereto, and were lost, as it were, in the hiding place.

Then we wrought there at felling timber and hewing, until we had bridged the river and made a causeway through the peat to Stanmoor hill, and then began to make a triple line of earthworks around its summit. No carelessly-built fort was this, for the king said: "If the nobles build badly, there will be excuse for every churl to do the like hereafter. Therefore this must needs be the most handsomely-wrought fort in all Wessex."

There came to us at this fort many faithful workmen, sent from the towns and countryside, until we had a camp there. But every night, after working with us and cheering all with his voice and example, Alfred went back to Athelney with us; and none would seek to disturb him there, so that for long none quite knew, among the lesser folk, where he bided. Presently the queen and athelings came there to him, and were safe.

That time in the fens was not altogether unpleasant, though the life was hard. Ever was Alfred most cheerful, singing and laughing as we wrought, and a word of praise from him was worth more than gold to every man. And then there were the hunting, the fishing, and the snaring of wild fowl, that were always on hand to supply our wants, though now we had plenty of food from the Quantock side. I know this, that many a man who was in Athelney with Alfred was the better therefor all the days of his after life. Men say that there is a steadfast look in the faces of the Athelney thanes, by which they can be well known by those who note the ways of men.

The frost lasted till February went out in rain and south winds. And then the Danes began to gather along the southern hills, watching us. By that time we had made causeways to other islets from the fort, and the best of these was to Othery, a long, flat island that lay to the east, nearer to the Polden Hills and Edington.

So one day the king sent for me as we wrought at the fort, and both he and I were horny handed and clay stained from the work. I came with spade in hand, and he leaned on a pick. Whereat he laughed.

"Faith, brother king, now can I speak in comrade's wise to my churls as you speak to your seamen. Nor do I think that I shall be the worse ruler for that."

Then he took my arm, and pointed to Edington hill.

"For many nights past I have seen watch fires yonder," he said; "and that is a place where I might strike the Danes well. So I would draw them thither in force. Do you feel as if a fight would be cheerful after this spade work?"

Now I could wish for nothing better, and I said so.

"Well, then," he went on, laughing at my eagerness, "go to Ethelnoth, and take twenty men, and do you and he fall on that post from Othery by night; and when you have scattered it, come back into the fen. I would have you lose no men, but I would make the Danes mass together by attack on some one point, and that as soon as may be, before Hubba comes. I do not want to hold their place."

Now that was the first of daily attacks on the Danish posts, at different places along the Selwood and Polden hills, until they thought that we wished to win Edington height, where we began and annoyed them most often. So I will tell how such a raid fared.

Good it was to lay aside pick and spade and take sword Helmbiter again, and don mail and helm; and I made Harek fence with me, lest I should have lost my sword craft through use of the weapons whereby the churl conquers mother earth. But once the good sword was in my hand I forgot all but the warrior's trade.

So Ethelnoth and I and twenty young thanes went in the evening to Othery island, and there found a fenman to guide us, and so went to the foot of Edington hill just as darkness fell. The watch-fire lights, that were our guide, twinkled above us through the trees that were on the hillside; and we made at once for them, sending on the fenman to spy out the post before we were near it. It was very dark, and it rained now and then.

When he came back to where we had halted, he said that there were about twenty tents, pitched in four lines, with a fire between each line; and that the men were mostly under cover, drinking before setting watch, if they set any at all.

So we drew nearer, skirting round into cover of some trees that came up to the tents, for the hilltop was bare for some way. The lighted tents looked very cheerful, and sounds of song and laughter came from them, and now and then a man crossed from one to another, or fed the fires with fresh wood, that hissed and sputtered as he cast it on.

"How shall we attack?" said Ethelnoth.

"Why, run through the camp in silence first and cut the tent lines, and then raise a war shout and come back on them. Then we may slay a few, and the rest will be scared badly enough."

Thereat we both laughed under our breath, for it seemed like a schoolboy's prank. Well, after the long toil in the fen, we were like boys just freed from school, though our game was the greatest of all--that of war--the game of Hodur's playground, as we Norse say.

Then I said:

"After we come through for the second time, we must take to this cover, and so get together at some place by the hill foot. There is a shed by a big tree that can be found easily."

So we passed the wood, and our comrades chuckled. It was good sport to see the shadows of the careless Danes on the tent walls, and to know that they dreamed of nothing less than that Saxons were on them. Four rows of tents there were, and there were twenty-two of us; so we told off men to each row, and then made for them at a moment when no man was about-- hacking at the ropes, and laughing to see the tents fall. It was strange to watch the shadows start up and stand motionless, as the first patter of feet came and the first blows fell, and then bustle, helpless and confused, with savage shouts and curses, as the heavy canvas and skins fell in upon them.

Now we were through the camp, and the outcries were loud behind us. Two or three tents did not fall, and from them the men swarmed, half armed and startled, not knowing if this was not some sorry jest at first; and then rang our war cry from the dark, and we were back upon them. We were but two-and-twenty to a hundred, but they knew not what was on hand, while we did; and so we cut through them without meeting with any hurt. Two tents were on fire and blazing high, and blackened men cut and tore their way out of them howling; and I think that more than one Dane was cut down by his comrades in the panic that fell on all.

Yet even as we passed into the cover and went our way back towards the fen, some bolder spirits began to rally, and a horn was blown. But we were gone, leaving six slain and many more wounded among them, while not one of us was scratched.

They did not follow us, and we heard the clamour we had caused going on for some time after we had gained the fen. Presently, too, when we reached Othery, we saw a fire signal lit to call for help, and we were well content. Doubtless those Danes waked under arms all that night through.

After that these attacks were seldom so easy, for the Danes kept good watch enough; but they were ever the same in most ways. Suddenly in the night would come the war cry and the wild rush of desperate men on some Danish outpost, and before they knew what to do we were away and into the fen again. We grew to know every path well before long, and sometimes we would fall on small parties of our foes when they were on the march or raiding the cattle, and cut through them, and get back to our fastness.

Once or twice we were followed in the grey of early morning; but few Danes ever got back from that pursuit. We would cut them off amid the peat bogs, or they would founder therein, and sink under the weight of armour.

Then they tried to force some fenmen they caught to guide them to us at Othery. Once the brave fenman led them to where they dared not move till daylight came, while the blue fen lights flitted round them like ghosts in the dark; and then the fen people swarmed round them, and ended them with arrows and sling stones from a distance. They tried no more night attacks on us after that. But again they came in some force by daylight, and we had a strange fight on a narrow strip of hard land in Sedgemoor, with all advantage on our side. No Danes won back to the Polden Hills.

Then they dared not try the fens any more, and daily we kept their sentries watching, and nightly we fell on outposts, until at last they thought our force grew very great, and began to gather on Edington hill, even as Alfred wished. And this saved many a village and farm and town from plunder, for the fear of Alfred the king began to grow among his foes.

Then the king made his next move; for, now that the way was open, he sent to Odda at Exeter, bidding him move up to Taunton by some northerly road, gathering what Devon men he could on the way. There is hardly a stronger town in Wessex than the great fortress that Ine the king made.

At this time I began to be full of thoughts about my ships. But they could hardly be built as yet; and most of them were in southern havens, whence, even were they ready, one could not bring them round the stormy Land's End in early March. Yet the weather was mild and open, and I began to think that at any time Hubba might bring his Danes across the narrow Severn sea to join his kinsmen at Edington. We heard, too, that Guthrum, the king of East Anglia, was there now, and that he had summoned every warrior who would leave the land he had won to come to him.

Men have blamed Guthrum for treachery in this; but seeing that the peace was broken, and that he must needs fight for the peace at least of his kingdom, I hold that this is not right. At all events, Alfred blamed him not in the time to come. Nevertheless, I suppose that in men's minds he always will be held answerable for what the other chiefs wrought of ill, because he bore the name of king from the first, and ruled East Anglia. No Saxon, who is used to hold his king as over all, will understand how little power a host-king of the north has.

Now all this while my good ship lay at Bridgwater, and with her were fifty of my men, who were well quartered among the townsfolk, and helped to guard the bridge. And, as I have said, two ships were being built there. So one day in the third week in March I rode away with Kolgrim from Athelney, to see how all things were going on there, meaning also to go to Heregar's place for a time, having messages to give him from the king.

Harek was coming with me; but Alfred asked me to spare him for this time.

"I have to learn somewhat from the scald," he said.

"Wizardry, my king?" I asked, laughing, for that was ever a jest at the scald's expense after it was known how we found out that Alfred was at Denewulf's house.

"Nay, but song," he answered. "Now I see not why I should not tell you who put the thought into my mind; but I am going, as you did, to spy out the Danish camp. And I will go as a gleeman, and be welcome enough as a Saxon who has enough love of Danes to learn some northern sagas for them!"

"My king," I cried, "this is too perilous altogether."

He looked quaintly at me.

"Go to, cousin; are you to have all the glory? If you went, why not I? Maybe I too may find a chance of helping some fair maiden on the way back."

Then I prayed him to do nothing rash, for that he was the one hope of England.

"And maybe the one man in England who can do any good by going, therefore," he answered. "And neither you nor I would ask any man to do for us what we durst not do ourselves."

"You will be known, my king," I said.

Whereon he held out his hands, which were hard and horny now with hard work, and he laughed as he did so.

"Look at those," he said, "and at my unkempt hair and beard! Verily I may be like Alfred the king in some ways, but not in these. They will pass me anywhere."

So I could not dissuade him, and ever as I tried to do so he waxed more cheerful, and made sport of me, throwing my own doings in my teeth, and laughing about Thora. So I was fain to get away from his presence, lest I should grow angry at last. And when I was going he said:

"Have no fear, cousin; I will not go unless I am well prepared."

So I went, and next day was back in Athelney, riding hard; for Hubba's ships had been sighted from the Quantocks, and they were heading for the Parret. What I looked for and feared was coming.

Then Alfred sent messengers to Odda, who had come to Taunton two days before this. And he gathered every man from the fen, and we went to Bridgwater, leaving our little force there, and so rode on the way to Combwich, thinking to see the sails of the ships in Bridgwater Bay. But a shift of wind had come, and they were yet over on the Welsh coast, waiting for the tide to enable them to come down on us.

By that time a fire burned on the highest spur of the Quantocks to tell us that Odda was there, and at once another was lit on the Combwich fort to bring him to us, for it seemed certain that here we must fight the first battle of Alfred's great struggle.

"Here you must meet this newcomer and drive him away, if it can be done, or if not, hinder him from coming further; or if that is impossible, do your best. I would have you remember that defeat here is not loss of all hope, for beyond Selwood lies our real gathering. But victory, even if dearly bought, will almost win the day for us."

So Alfred said, and we, who began to see what his great plan was, were cheered.

In the evening Odda came with eight hundred men of Devon. Alfred had two hundred maybe, and my few men and the townsfolk made another two hundred. But Hubba had twenty-three longships, whose crews, if up to fighting strength, would not be less than a hundred in each.

So we watched till the tide fell, when he could not come into the Parret, and then I went back to Heregar's hall. It seemed very bare, for all goods had been sent up to the great refuge camp of Dowsborough, to which all day long the poor folk had been flying, driving with them their sheep and cattle and swine, that they might save what they could. But with Odda had come his daughter, the Lady Etheldreda, who would not leave him; and she and the Lady Alswythe and Thora were yet in the house, and Osmund the jarl sat in the hall, listless and anxious of face. It was an ill time for him; but there were none of us who did not like him well, and feel for him in his helplessness.

"What news?" he said, when he saw me come into the hall.

"Hubba will be here on the next tide--with early morning," I said.

He sighed, and rising up went to the doorway and looked out to the hills.

"I would that I could make these two noble ladies seek refuge yonder," he said; "but one will not leave her father, nor the other her husband."

Then I said:

"At least I think you should take Thora there. This is a difficult place for you."

"I know Hubba," he said, "and if I abide here I may be of use. I need not tell you that you are fighting the best warrior of our time, and that with too small a force."

"Well," I said, "you and I can speak plainly, neither of us being Saxons. We shall be beaten by numbers, and you mean that you will be able to save these ladies by staying?"

"Ay," he said. "And if by any chance Alfred wins, I may be able to ask for mercy for the conquered."

Then came in Thora, and her face was troubled. She had been trying to make Etheldreda go to the hill fort, where all the women and children of the countryside had been sent.

"It is of no use," she said; "they will bide here."

"Well," said Osmund, "then we will stay also. I and our friend have spoken thereof, and it seems well that we do so."

I suppose they had talked of this before, for she made no answer, but sat down wearily enough before the fire; and Osmund and I went out to the courtyard, for we were both restless.

Then Heregar came in on his white horse, and saw Osmund, and called to him, asking of the same business, for he had asked the jarl to speak about it as a friend. So I went in again, and Thora sat by herself yet, looking up to see who came now. I went and stood by her, staring into the fire, and feeling as if I wanted to go out again. Restlessness was in the very air while we waited for the coming fight.

"King Ranald," she said, after a little silence, "I wonder if ever a maiden was in such sad doubt as I. I cannot wish that these dear ladies, who have made a friend of me, should see their folk beaten, and maybe slain; and cannot wish that my own kin should be beaten either. It seems that in either way I must find heavy sorrow."

That was true; but it was certain that her own people were the cause of all the trouble, though I could not say so. I put it this way:

"I think that if your people are driven off there will be peace the sooner, and maybe they will not land when they find us waiting. I know, too, that those who have loved ones in the battle that may be are in a harder case than yours, dear lady."

Then she looked up at me once, and a flush came slowly over her pale face, and she answered nothing. I thought that she felt some shame that a warrior like her father should bide here, without moving hand or foot, when the war horns were blowing. So I said:

"Harder yet would it be if the jarl were in the battle against our friends. Then would the fear of his loss be a terror to you also."

Now came in Osmund, and straightway Thora rose up, turning away from us both, and went from the hall. The jarl looked after her curiously and sadly.

"This is a strange business for the girl," he said.

"She seems almost as troubled because you are not fighting as if you were in danger by doing so," I answered, with that thought still in my mind.

Thereat the jarl stared at me.

"What has put that into your head?" he asked.

I told him what she and I had said, adding that I feared I had seemed to hint somewhat discomforting.

Then said Osmund, looking in my face with a half smile:

"She is glad I am honourably out of this business, and the trouble is not that. There are one or two, maybe, whom she would like to see as safe in the same way."

Then it flashed through my dull mind that perhaps I was one of these, and the thought was pleasant to me.

"Well," I said, "there are the thane, and his young son, the king's page, who is here. They have been very kind to her."

"Also a wandering king who took her out of danger," he said then.

"Ay; I shall be glad if she thinks of me."

There were a little laugh and a rustling behind us, and one said:

"Either you are the least conceited of men or the blindest, King Ranald, or you would know what is amiss."

I turned, and saw the Lady Etheldreda herself, and I bowed to her in much confusion.

"O you men!" she said. "Here you will let the poor girl break her heart in silence, while you fight for glory, or somewhat you think is glory, without a word to say that you care that she shall see what you win. Of course she thinks of you, even night and day. How else should it be, when you have been as a fairy prince to her?"

Then I knew for myself that among all the wild life of Athelney and the troubles of the king the thought of Thora had been pleasant to me; but now I was confused, having the matter brought home to me suddenly, and, as it were, before I was ready to shape all my thoughts towards her. So all that I could say was foolish enough.

"I am a poor sort of fairy prince, lady."

"Ay," she said; "I am as good a fairy godmother, maybe. And perhaps I should have said nothing--at this time. But, Ranald, the maiden weeps for your danger, for, at the very least, she owes you much."

Then I said, humbly as I felt:

"That is more honour to me than I deserve."

"That is for her to say," answered the fair lady, turning to where Osmund had been.

But he was now in the doorway, looking out again to the hills. So she was silent, and I thought of somewhat.

"There is none in this land or in any other--of whom I think as I do of Thora," I said; "but my mind has been full of warfare and trouble with the king. Now, if I may, I will ask for somewhat that I may wear for her sake in the fight, and so she will know that I think of her."

"Now that is well said," answered Etheldreda. "But you must ask it for yourself."

Thereat I thought for a moment, and at last I said that I would not do so.

"If I might, I would ask you to gain this favour for me," I said; "for I think that a parting would be very hard, as things have come about."

"You are a wiser man than I thought you, Ranald," she said; and so she went from me, and I stayed by the fire, thinking thoughts that were sweet and yet troublous, for beyond tomorrow's fight I could not see.

Then the lady came back, and with her she brought a little glove, worn and shapely from the hand that it belonged to.

"She bids me give this to her king and warrior," Etheldreda said. "I did but tell her that you asked a token that she minded you."

"It was well," I answered. "What said she?"

"Nought at once. But her sadness went, and her face changed--ay, but she is beyond any of us in beauty when her eyes light up in that way--and she fetched this, and then said 'Say, if you think that he will care to know it, that this is the glove wherein I rode to Wareham.'

"Do you care to know it, Ranald?"

"Ay, with all my heart," I said.

And so I put it very carefully under the broad, golden-studded baldric of Sigurd's sword. And it would not stay there, and Etheldreda laughed at me, and took a little golden brooch like a cross that she wore, and pinned it through glove and baldric, making all safe.

"There," she said, "is a token from me also, though it was unasked. Bear yourself well, Ranald, for our eyes are on you. If Hubba comes indeed, we women folk will be in the fort."

Then I said, being at a loss for words enough:

"I would I had the tongue of Harek the scald, that I might thank you for gift and words, my fairy princess."

"I have half a mind to take it back for that fine saying," she answered.

And then she gave me her hand, and I kissed it; and she went from me with her eyes full of tears for all the trouble that was on us, though she had tried bravely to carry it off lightly.

Then I would stay in the house no longer, but went out to the fort, and sat down by the great Dragon banner of Wessex, Heregar's charge, that floated there, and ate and drank with the other chiefs, and waited. But my mind was full of what I had heard, and the war talk went on round me without reaching my ears.

Chapter XI. The Winning of "The Raven."

Now we none of us like much to speak of the fight that came next morning, for it went ill enough. Yet we were outnumbered by twice our force, for some more of the host beyond the fens made Alfred send many of his men back to watch the crossing at Bridgwater.

Hubba brought his ships up on the tide, and when he saw that we were waiting for him, he made as if to go on up the river; and we began to move from our position, thinking that he would go and fall on the town. Then, very suddenly, he turned his ships' bows to the bank at the one place where he saw that the land was high almost to the river's edge; and before we knew that we must be there to stay him, his men were ashore, and had passed the strip of marsh, and were on a long, gentle rise that ends in Cannington hill and the Combwich fort, half a mile away.

We fought well for an hour, and then our men began to give on either wing, for they were, as I would have it remembered, raw levies that Odda had brought with him--valiant men and strong, but with no knowledge of how to fight in line or how to hold together. And when a force like that begins to go, it is ended.

Hard fought we in the centre after that. There were the Athelney thanes, and my fifty men, and Odda's Exeter and Taunton townsfolk, who had fought before; but when the wings broke, Hubba's great force of veterans lapped round us, and we had nought left us but to cut our way out, and make the best retreat we could. My men shouted as they struck, in our Norse way; but a deadly silence fell on the Saxons, and I thought that, as they grew quiet, their blows became ever more stern and fell, until at last even Hubba's vikings gave way before the hard-set faces and steadfast eyes of the west-country spearmen, whom no numbers seemed to daunt, and they drew back from us for a space.

Then we were clear of them, and at once Ethelnoth closed in on the king, taking his horse's rein, and praying him to fly to Bridgwater, where a stand could be made. And at last he persuaded him, and they turned. Then fearing that this might set the example for general flight, I spoke to Odda, and we shouted to the men to stand fast and hold back pursuit; and so a guard of some fifty thanes went with Alfred, and we faced the Danes even yet.

They saw what was done, and roared, and charged on us; and we began to retreat slowly, fighting all the way, up the long slope of land towards the fort. But I saw Heregar's horse rear and fall, and the banner went down, and I thought him slain in that attack.

Presently they let us go. We won ever to better ground, and they had to fight uphill; and then we gained the fort, and there they durst not come.

Then rode towards me a man in silver armour that was dinted and hacked--shieldless, and with a notched sword in his hand. It was Heregar.

"I thought you slain, friend," I said gladly.

"Would that I were! for my charge is lost; they have my banner," he answered.

"That may be won back yet," I said. "But there is no shame to you; we were outnumbered by more than two to one."

"I have borne it through ten battles," he said, and that was all; but he put his face in his hands and groaned.

Now I looked out over the field we had left, and saw the Danes scattering in many ways. Some were going in a long line up the steep hill beyond which the village lay, and over this line swayed and danced the lost banner. There was a crowd of our men from the broken wings gathered there--drawn together by the king as he fled, as I knew afterwards; and I think the Danes bore our banner with them in order to deceive them. I knew that the lane was deep and hollow up which they must go, and there were woods on either side.

Whereat I sprang up.

"Thane," I said, "here is a chance for us to win back the banner, as I think."

He looked up sharply, and I pointed.

"Let us ride at once into the wood, and wait for them to pass us. Then, if we dare, we can surely dash through them."

Kolgrim sat close to me, and our horses were tethered to a spear. He rose up when he heard me speak, saying:

"Here is more madness. But trust to Ranald's luck, thane."

Then in a few more minutes we were riding our hardest towards the wood. I heard Odda shout after us from the entrance to the fort as we went, but we heeded him not.

We edged up to the deep lane through the trees until we were so near that we could almost see into it. The banner was at the head of the column, and there were no mounted men with it. Hubba had brought no horses with him from across the sea.

Then we waited for a long minute, hearing the tramp of the coming men, and their loud talk and laughter as they boasted of their prize. They were going very carelessly.

"If we get it," I whispered to the thane, whose eyes were shining, "ride hard up the hill to our folk who are there."

He nodded and then before us fluttered the folds of his treasure. Instantly he spurred his great white horse, and leaped straight at it into the lane, and after him on either side came Kolgrim and I.

A great howl rose from the startled Danes, and I saw Heregar wheel his horse and tear the banner from the man who held it, cutting down another warrior who tried to catch his bridle. Then Helmbiter was hard at work for a moment, and Kolgrim's axe rattled on a helm or two; and we were away up the lane before the shouting and confusion were over, none of the Danes knowing but that more of us would follow from out the cover.

One or two arrows, shot by men who found their wits sooner than the rest, pattered after us, and we gained the hilltop and the great cheer that went up from our few men who were there made the Danes halt and waver, and at last turn back to the open again.

We stayed on that hilltop for an hour. Then the Danes were coming up in force, and there was no hope in staying, so we got back to the fort before they could cut us off.

Soon after this there was a general movement on the part of our foes, and before evening we were surrounded on all sides by strong posts, and it was plain that we were not to move from the fort.

Now this is not very large, but it is very strong--the hill which has been fortified being some two hundred feet high, and steep sided as a house roof on all sides but the east, where the entrance must needs be. But this again has outworks; and the road into the ramparts from the long slope of Cannington hill to the southward runs slantwise through them, so that the gap it makes in the first line is covered by the second. And both upper and lower rampart go right round the circle of the hilltop, and are very strong, having been made by the British folk, who well understood such matters, and had such fighters as the old Romans and our own forefathers to deal with. Some parts of the works were of piled stones, and the rest of earth, as the ground required.

There is but one way in which that fort could be taken by force, as I think, and that is by attacking on all sides at once, which needs a greater force than would ever be likely to come against it. Moreover, on one side the marshy course of the Combwich stream would hinder any heavy onslaught.

So inside these ramparts were we with some six hundred men, and there we were watched by three times our number. There was a strong post on Cannington hill, between us and Bridgwater; another--and that the main body--between us and the ships, on a little, sharp hill crest across a stony valley two bowshots wide that lay between it and the fort; and so we were well guarded.

At first this seemed of little moment, for we were to stay Hubba before the place; and for a while there was nothing but rejoicing over the return of the banner. Then I found there was no water in the place, and that we had but what food each man happened to carry with him. Presently that want of water became terrible, for our wounded began to cry for it piteously. Maybe it was as well that we had few with us, because the field was left in the hands of the Danes.

Up and down among those few went Etheldreda and Alswythe and Thora, tending them and comforting them, where we had sent them--to the highest point of the hilltop, inside the upper rampart; and I could see the flutter of their dresses now and then from where I watched beside Odda on the lower works. I had spoken to neither since we came here.

Towards dusk I spoke to Odda, and he gave me twenty men; and gathering all the vessels of any sort that would hold water, we climbed over the rampart next the marsh, and stole down to the nearest pool and brought back all we could, using helms and leathern cloaks and the like, for want of buckets. We got back safely that time, and I sent the same men again, thinking that there was no danger, and so not going myself.

They got back, indeed, but with a party of Danes after them; and but for our arrow flights from the earthworks, they would have had to fight, and lose what they brought. After that Hubba knew what we needed, and sent a strong picket to keep us from the marsh.

So the night passed and we had some hopes that a force might come to our help from Bridgwater in the morning, for it was possible that the king would be able to gather men there. It was a slender hope, though, for the host on Polden Hills had to be watched.

All day we waited, and no help came; and with evening the last food had gone. It had rained heavily, however, and the want of water was past for the time. The Danes never moved from their places, waiting to starve us out; and in the last light of evening a small party came across the little valley from the main body, bearing a white flag in token of parley. Hubba bid us yield, and our lives should be spared.

"It is good of Hubba to give us the chance of living a little longer," answered Odda; "but we will wait here a while, so please him."

The Danes threatened us, and mocked, and so went back. We had no more messages from their chief after that.

That night we slept round the standard where it flapped on the hilltop. The men watched, turn by turn, along the lower ramparts; and the Danes were not so near that we could be surprised by them, for there was no cover to hide their coming. Nestled under the northwest rampart was a little hut--some shepherd's shelter where the three poor ladies were bestowed. Osmund the jarl sat a little apart from us, but all day and night he had been tending the wounded well. Harek who, as befitted a scald, was a good leech, said that the jarl knew almost as much of the craft as he.

Now, in the early morning, when the light was grey, I woke, hearing the rattle of arms and the quiet passing of the word as the men changed guard, and I thought I would go round the ramparts; and then Odda woke also. The rest slept on, for they had taken their turns on watch-- Heregar with his arm round the pole of the standard, and his sword beneath his head.

Odda looked at me as we sat up stiffly, and spoke what was in his mind and mine also.

"I have a mind to send Osmund to Hubba, and ask him to let the women go hence. There is nought to eat today."

"There is enough kept for them," I said; for Heregar had seen to that, and none had grudged a share.

"Ay," he answered; "but what are we to do? Are we to be starved like rats here?"

"There are the half-dozen horses," I said.

"And nought to cook them withal. I would that the king would come."

"It is in my mind that he cannot," I answered; "there has been some move of the other host."

Now that was true, for Guthrum's great following had suddenly swept down towards Bridgwater, and that could not be left. They were camped now at the foot of the hill, watching there as Hubba watched us.

Then some one came, stepping lightly, but with clank of mail, towards us; and I glanced round, thinking that some message was brought from the ramparts. Odda turned idly at the same time, and he started up.

"Ah!" he said, under his breath, "what is this?"

A tall maiden, mail clad and bearing a broad-bladed spear, stood beside us; and I thought her one of the Valkyrias--Odin's messengers--come to us, to fight for us in some strife to which she would lead us. I rose too, saluting.

"Skoal to the shield maiden!" I said.

"Skoal to the heroes!" she answered; and then I knew the voice, though, under the helm and in the grey light, the face of the ealdorman's daughter Etheldreda had been strange to me. And Odda knew also.

"What would you in this guise, my daughter?" he cried.

"I think that I have come as Ranald thought--as a Valkyria to lead you to battle," she answered, speaking low, that she might not wake the tired warriors around her. "There is but one thing for us to do, and that is to die sword in hand, rather than to perish for want of food and water here."

I know that this had been in my mind, and most likely in Odda's also; but Alfred might come.

"We wait the king," the ealdorman said.

"No use," she answered. "One may see all the Polden Hills from this place, and tonight there are no fires on Edington height, where we have been wont to see them."

Odda groaned. "My Etheldreda, you are the best captain of us all," he said.

Then suddenly Heregar rose up on his elbow from beside the standard, crying strangely:

"Ay, Father Eahlstan--when the tide is low. Somerset and Dorset side by side. What say you, father--Somerset and Devon? Even so."

The other sleepers stirred, and the lady turned and looked on the thane, but he slept even yet.

"Heregar dreams of the bishop he loved, and of the great fight they fought yonder and won thirty rears ago," she said [lxv].

"Worn out is the brave thane," said I. "Strange dreams come to one when that is so."

Then Heregar woke, and saw the maiden, and rose up at her side.

"Dear lady," he asked, "what is this?"

"Ranald thought me a Valkyria, friend; and I come on a Valkyria's errand."

"I had a strange dream but now," Heregar said, as if it dwelt in his mind, so that he hardly heeded what Etheldreda answered him. "I thought that Bishop Eahlstan stood by me as in the old days, and minded me of words that I spoke long ago, words that were taught me by a wise woman, who showed me how to trap the Danes, when the tide left their ships aground, so that they had no retreat. Then he said, 'Even again at this time shall victory be when the tide is low.' And I said that Somerset and Dorset would fail not at this time. Then said he, 'Somerset and Devon.' Then it seemed that he blessed me and passed. Surely I think that he would tell us that victory is before us."

Now the other sleepers woke, and listened wondering. The light was strong, and I looked away towards the Danes between us and the river. Their fires were burning up one by one as they roused also; but I thought there was some bustle down at the shore of the river, where the ships were now afloat on the rising tide.

Then Etheldreda spoke to us in words that were brave and good to hear--words to make a man long to give his life for country and for friends--telling us that, since we must needs die, it was well that we should fall sword in hand, ridding England of her foes man to man, rather than perish in this place for nought.

And when she ended the chiefs were silent, looking on the Danes with eyes that gleamed; and Kolgrim put the thoughts of all into words when he said:

"Once or twice has the Berserker fury come on me when my master has been in peril. Berserker again will you drive me, lady, so that I care not for six foemen against me or sixty."

Then Odda cried:

"What goes on yonder? Do they leave us?" and he shaded his eyes against the rising sun, and pointed. Certainly the Danes were drawing towards the ships in parties of twenty and thirty at a time, but their sentries went on their beats without heeding them. There was no movement, either, among those on the other hill, and the Raven banner that told of Hubba's presence was not borne away.

Now we forgot all but that here was a new hope for us, and we watched for half an hour.

Then it was plain that full half the force was drawn off, and that the Danes were crossing the river in the ships. We saw them land on the opposite shore, where the road comes down to the Combwich crossing, that can only be used at lowest tides; and they marched eastward, doubtless in search of cattle and plunder.

Then Heregar's eyes shone, and he said:

"Now has our time come, even as Eahlstan foretold to me. In two hours or three none of that force can return, and we have but half as many again as ourselves left here for us to deal with."

"Let me lead you on them," said Etheldreda.

Then with one voice we prayed her to bide in the fort, and for long she would not be persuaded. But we told her that the men would fight as well under her eye as if they were led by her--if, indeed, her presence did not weaken them, in fear for her safety--and so at last she gave way.

After that there was no more doubt as to what should be done; but Odda went round among the men, and spoke to them in such wise that he stirred their hearts to die bravely hand to hand with the Danes. And I thought that some of us might live to see a great if dearly-bought victory; for it was certain that not one of these Saxons but meant to die before he left the field.

Then Heregar and Osmund went with Etheldreda to the other two ladies, and they bade them take the horses and fly to Dowsborough camp as soon as the fighting drew every Dane to the eastward side of the fort and left the way clear. Osmund would go with them, and so no fear for them was on our minds.

Then we got the soundest of the wounded down to the lower rampart, and drew off the men there towards the gateway, so that the Danes might think our movement was but a changing of guard; then we waited until we saw that the ships on the far bank had taken the ground.

Then we sallied out, and as I went I looked back once. Three women stood alone on the hilltop, and one waved to us. That was the Valkyria, for her mail sparkled in the sun; but I had eyes only for that one whom I thought I should not see again, whose little glove was on my heart.

Now, if we were desperate, Odda was not the man to waste any chance of victory that there might be. We went swiftly up the long slope of Cannington hill, and fell on the post there before they on the main guard could reach them. There was no withstanding the terrible onset of our Saxons; half that force was slain, and the rest were in full flight in a few minutes.

Then we went steadily down the hill to where Hubba himself waited for us. His war horns were blowing, to call in every man who was within hearing; and his men were formed in line four deep at the foot of the spur on which their camp had been.

Now, when I saw this I looked on our men, who were in column again; and it seemed to me that the old Norse plan would be good, for it was certain that on this field we meant to stay.

"Ealdorman," I said, "while there is yet time let us form up in a wedge and go through that line. Then shall we fight back to back, and shall have some advantage. I and my men, who have axes, will go first."

Then my few vikings cried, "Ay, king!" and shouted; whereat Odda laughed grimly.

"Go on, Berserker--axes must needs lead--we will do it."

Then we changed the ranks quickly, and I and Kolgrim and Harek made the point of that wedge. Heregar and the banner were in the midst, and Odda himself was not far behind me, putting his best men along the two foremost faces of the wedge.

"We shall not be foremost long," I said; "we shall be surrounded when once we are through the line."

But as we came on, Hubba closed up his men into a dense, square mass.

"Ho!" said Harek to me; "you are wrong, my king."

Now we were close at hand, and the Danish arrows flew among us, and the javelins fell pretty thickly. I think that a wedge bears this better than any other formation, for it is easy to stop the weapons that reach it.

Our men were silent now, and I was glad, having known already what that meant; but the Danes began to yell their war cries. Then we were within ten paces of them, and I gripped shield and axe and gave the word to charge, and Odda answered it.

Then was such a terrible roar from the Saxons as I had never heard--the roar of desperate men who have their foes before them, more awful than any war shout. And at that even the vikings shrank a little, closing their ranks, and then, with all the weight of the close-ranked wedge behind me, we were among them, and our axes were at work where men were driven on one another before us; and the press thinned and scattered at last, while the Danes howled, and for a moment we three and a few lines behind us stood with no foemen before us, while all down the sides of the wedge the fight raged. Then we halted, and the Danes lapped round us. I do not know that we lost more than two men in this first onset, so heavy was it; but the Danes fell everywhere.

Now began fighting such as I had heard of, but had never seen before. The scalds sing of men who fought as fights a boar at bay in a ring of hounds, unfearing and silent; and so fought we. My axe broke, and I took to sword Helmbiter, and once Kolgrim went Berserker, and howled, and leaped from my side into a throng which fell on us, and drove them back, slaying three outright, and meeting with no hurt.

Our wedge held steady. Men fell, but we closed up; and there grew a barrier of slain before us. I had not seen Hubba since we first closed in, and then he had been a little to the right of where we struck his line, under a golden banner, whereon was a raven broidered, that hung motionless in the still morning air.

Presently the Danish onslaught slackened. Men were getting away from their line to the rear, worn out or wounded, and the hill beyond them was covered with those who had fallen out. They had beaten against our lines as one beats on a wall--hewing out stones, indeed, but without stirring it. They had more hurt than we.

Odda pushed to my side, and said to me:

"What if we advance towards the hill crest?"

"Slowly, then," I said.

He passed the word, and we began to move, and the Danes tried to stay us. Then their attack on the rear face of the wedge slackened and ceased, and they got round before us to fight from the higher ground. At once Odda saw that an attack in line as they wavered thus would do all for us, so he swung his hard Devon levies to right and left on us Norsemen as the centre--maybe there were twenty of us left at that time--and as the wings swung forward with a rolling cheer, the Danes crumbled away before them, and we drove them up the little hill and over the brow, fighting among the half-burnt watch fires and over heaps of plunder, even to where the tall "Raven" drooped from its staff.

Then I saw the mighty Hubba before me; and had I not known it already, one might see defeat written in his face as he looked across to his ships. His men were back now, and stood on the far shore, helpless. Then was a cheer from our left, and he looked there, and I looked also.

Out of the fort came our wounded--every one who could put one foot before another--a strange and ghastly crowd of fifty or sixty men who would yet do what they might for England. And with them was a mixed crowd of thralls and village folk, bearing what arms they could find on the place whence we drove the first Danes, and forks, and bill hooks, and heavy staves.

I do not know if the Danes saw what manner of force came to our help; but I think they did not. Many broke and fled to the ships; but Hubba's face grew hard and desperate, and he cried to his men to stand, and they gathered round him and the Raven banner.

Once again our great wedge formed up, and again charged into the thick of the Danes. Then I faced the great chief, and men fell back from us to see what fight should be. But from beside me came Odda.

"My fight, Ranald," he said, and strode before the Dane.

His sword was gone--the hilt and three inches of blade hung from his wrist--and his shield was notched and gashed. His only weapon was the broad-bladed Saxon spear, ashen shafted, with iron studs along its length below the head. He was a head shorter than the Dane, who was, in truth, the most splendid warrior I had ever seen; and he bore a broad axe, wedge beaten and gold inlaid. There was not much to choose between his shield and Odda's, but I thought the spear the weaker weapon.

"Axe against spear," said Harek; "here is somewhat of which to sing."

Once Odda feinted, lunging at Hubba's face; and the Dane raised his shield a little, but did not move else, nor did his eyelids so much as flinch, and his steady look never left his foe's face. Then, as Odda recovered, the great axe flashed suddenly, and fell harmless as its mark sprang back from its sweep; while like light the spear point went forward over the fallen axe, that recovered too slowly to turn it, and rang true on the round shield that met it.

I had not thought much of spear play until now, for we think little of the weapon.

Again the Saxon lunged, and Hubba hewed at the spear shaft, splintering it a little as the quick-eyed spearman swung it away from the blow. Then the butt was over Odda's left shoulder, and before one could tell that its swing aside had ended, forward flew the point, darting from left to right over Hubba's arm that had not yet recovered from the lost axe blow, and behind the shield's rim. That blow went home, and the mighty Dane reeled and fell.

One moment's silence, and then a howl from the Danes who watched, and they flew on us, bearing us back a pace or two. Odda went down under the rush that was made on him, and I called to my comrades, and stood over him, and beat them back. But Hubba's fall was the end.

Even as I stood there, there came a rash of men from our ranks past me; and I cheered, for

I saw Heregar's silver mail driving straight for the Raven standard, at the head of the young thanes who were the shield wall of the Dragon of Wessex. Then, too, closed in the wounded men and the country folk; and the Danes broke and fled towards the ships in disorder. We followed for a little way, and then the thralls ended matters. They say that not one Dane reached the river's bank, beyond which their comrades watched and raged, powerless to help them.

I went back to where Odda had fallen, and at that time there rose a thundering cheer of victory from our wearied line, and helms were cast into the air, and weapons waved in wild joy. That roused one who lay before me, and white and shaking, up rose Odda from among the slain. I went to him, and got my arm round him; and again the men cheered, and little by little the colour came back to his face.

"I thought you slain outright," I said; "are you much hurt?"

"I cannot tell," he said. "I believe I am sound in limb, but my wind is gone. It is ill for a stout man to have mail-clad Danes hurled on him by heavy-handed vikings."

So he said, gasping, but trying to laugh. And, indeed, he was unwounded, save for a cut or two, and he still grasped his red spear in his right hand.

Now I looked on our men, and saw that we might not bide for another fight. Already some whom the wild joy of battle had kept strong in spite of wounds were falling among their comrades, and it seemed to me that wounds were being bound up everywhere.

But there was a token of victory that made these seem as nothing. In the midst of all Heregar stood with the Dragon banner, and by his side his son-in-law, Turkil the thane of Watchet, bore the captured "Raven."

Harek the scald looked at it once, and then went to its heavy folds, and scanned carefully the runes that were thereon.

"Ho, comrades!" he cried joyfully, "here is a winning that will be sung of long after our names are forgotten. This is the magic Raven that was wrought with wizardry and spells by the daughters of Ragnar Lodbrok. Ill will this news fall on Danish ears from end to end of England. This is worth two victories."

"I have seen it many times before," said Heregar; "nor is this the only time that I have tried to win it. But never before have I seen it hanging motionless as it hung today. There seems to be somewhat in the tale they tell of its flapping foreboding victory."

"Ay," said Odda. "Today they despised us, and bore it not forward; therefore it flapped not, seeing that there was no wind where it hung."

The ealdorman called us together then, and pointed to the Danes who were massed beyond the river.

"Now it is time for us to go. We have won a good fight, and some of us are yet alive. It will not be well to lose all by biding here to be slain to the last man now. Shall we go to Bridgwater or to the Quantocks, and so to Taunton?"

Then Heregar said:

"To the hills; for we should be penned in Bridgwater between this force and the other. I think that while we are yonder they will not do much on this side the Parret; and men will ever gather to us."

Then we took our wounded and went back to the fort--four hundred men out of six hundred who sallied out, where we thought that none would return. But how many Danes we left on the field it is hard to say. Some say six hundred, and some more; and it may be so. Their graves are everywhere over the hill where they fell. When the tide rose we were gone; and Hubba's men sought the body of their chief, and raised a mound over it. But they had no mind to stay on our side of the river, and they went to the Polden Hills, and laid the land waste far and wide, even to holy Glastonbury, until they joined Guthrum's force at Edington.

Now one may know in what wise Etheldreda the brave shield maiden met us, as we came back from that hard-won field, with words of praise and thanks. But Thora stood not with her as we passed through the fort gates, where she waited on the rampart with the Lady Alswythe. Nor had she watched the fight at all, being torn with sorrow and fear alike.

I found her presently, while the men made litters whereon to bear our wounded to safety, having cleansed the stains of war from my armour. King Harald's mail had kept me from wound worth notice--though, indeed, I hardly know how it was that I was unhurt thus. Kolgrim would not use his arm for many days, and Harek was gashed in arm and thigh also.

When Osmund heard my tread, he started up from where he sat beside Thora, looking away towards the hills to which we were going, and greeted me warmly.

"It was a good fight, Ranald, and well won," he said.

Then Thora turned slowly, and looked at me fearfully, as if she feared me. I was grieved, and would have gone away; but she drew nearer, and the fear went from her eyes when she saw that I was safe, knowing little of what I had been through. And at last she smiled faintly, saying:

"King Ranald, they say my warrior has fought well."

"It had been strange had I not, Thora," I said.

"I think I should have hated my own kin had you fallen," she said then.

"Ay," said Osmund, "war sees strange chances, and a man's thoughts are pulled in many ways. Many a time have I seen Dane fight with Dane on the old shores; and I can welcome a victor heartily, even if it is my own kin who have been beaten. Presently we Danes will fight for our new homes in England against such a landing from beyond seas as you have met."

There was some scratch on my shield arm that drew Thora's eyes at this time, and as the jarl spoke she came quickly to me, taking some light scarf she had from her dress at the same moment.

"You are hurt," she said; "though it is little. Let me bind it for you."

I suffered her to do so, saying nothing, but smiling at her, while the colour came brightly into her face as she wrought. The jarl smiled also, turning away presently as some new shouting came up from the fort gateway, where men welcomed those who bore back the spoils from the slain.

Then Thora had finished, and I put my arm round her and kissed her once.

"My lady," I said, "it was worth the wound that you should tend it."

And so she looked up at me frankly, and we knew well what had grown up between us since the day when we had ridden together into Wareham streets.

Chapter XII. Edington Fight.

Now after this we held the great Dowsborough fort on Quantocks for a few days, looking out over the land that should see the greatest deeds of Alfred, the wise king, from Glastonbury in the east to the wide stretches of the great wood, Selwood Forest, beyond the Stanmoor fens; and there, in the clear air, and with plenty of good provender from the smiling Taunton vale behind us, we grew strong again.

The Danes marched on Bridgwater, and the garrison must needs leave the place and retreat to the heights at Petherton, and there hide. I was grieved that my good ship was in Danish hands, but at least I knew that they would not harm her; and such was our faith in Alfred the king, that I believed that I should have her back. Old Thord came up to us when his charge was thus lost.

"Maybe they will finish painting her, and we shall be able to launch her, when we go back, without more trouble," he said. "Two of Hubba's ships, moreover, are worth having."

Then the king rode up to us, and told us that we had done well, and that the great plan yet held. Already he had messengers out throughout all the southern counties, and already men were gathering through the land and filling the towns that the Danes were leaving.

"When I know that the Danes have their eyes fixed on Quantock side again, I shall strike," he said.

So began again the life in Athelney and at Stanmoor fort; but now the Devon men gathered openly on our hills, and every day the Danish force grew also. When the last fight came, there would be an end to either one side or the other, and Guthrum knew it.

Once in that time I rode with Alfred, and saw Neot again; and if it were but for a few hours that we might stay with him, he found time to speak with me, asking if I had learned aught of his faith as yet.

"I have been in Athelney," I answered, "and I saw what might the holy Name has at Chippenham. The old gods have passed from me."

Little have I said of this, for one cannot speak of inmost thoughts; but so it was. Yet I think that, had I been older, the old faith would have died more slowly from my mind. So it was also with Harek the scald, but I think that he was Christian in heart before I had bent my mind to the matter in earnest. Long talks had he with Denewulf, the wise herdsman, while I listened.

So holy Neot rejoiced greatly over us, bidding me seek baptism at once.

"Nay, father," I said; "I fear it, knowing what it is. Let me bide for a time till I am stronger in these deep things."

He tried to persuade me gently, but at last let me be, knowing that I spoke in earnest and with all wish to seek it rightly.

So we left him on the day after we came, and went back to Athelney, and Alfred was very silent all the way.

"What ails you, my king?" I asked him at last, fearing that his pain, which had left him of late altogether, might return.

"I will tell you, cousin," he said. "Plainly has Neot shown me that all these troubles have come from my own pride and self will when first I was king. It is a long chain of happenings, of which you would know nought were I to try to tell you. But so it has been, and I weep therefor in my very heart."

Then said I:

"What is past is past, King Alfred, and best friend. Look on to the days to come, for I think that there shall rise a new and happier England before the winter comes again. There is no man whom I have met in all the hosts in whose heart is not love and best thoughts of you. Old days are forgotten as if they had never been, save that you led and conquered in the great battles beyond the Thames."

He held out his hand to me, and took mine and gripped it, saying no word, and riding on in silence for a mile and more. And after that he was of good cheer again till we came to Exeter, and there I stayed to see how fared my ships, for it was time they were in the water again.

Well had my men and the Saxon wrights wrought at building. If all went like this, King Alfred would have a fleet that could sweep the seas from Dover to Orme's Head, and keep his land from new plunderers at least.

In a week I came back to Athelney, and there was good cheer, and all were in the best of heart, for things went well. Messengers came and went across the winding paths from the southern hills, and Ethered met me laughing, and said:

"The king has robbed you of your glory, Ranald. He has been into the Danish camp--even to the presence of Guthrum himself."

Then I would hear of this from Alfred himself.

"Ay," he said, when he had greeted me and heard that the ships were almost ready, "I have outdone you; for I have played the gleeman as I planned, and have been in the midst of them yonder on Edington hill."

"It was an awesome risk to run, my king," I said.

"Which you taught me yourself, cousin. Howbeit I met no damsel, and I had no companion to return with but him with whom I went--Heregar's young son, my page. Thane is he now by right of unfearing service. Once, when I climbed the hill, I began to fear greatly, and I stayed, and asked the boy if he was afraid to go on. Tell me truly, Ranald, did you fear when you were in Wareham?"

"Truly I feared at first," I answered; "but since I was there when it came on me, I must even go through with the business. So it passed."

"Well, I am glad you confess it," he answered, "for I was minded to turn and run when the first lights of the great camp showed through the trees. Then the boy answered me, 'My king, why should I fear when you are with me?' I was ashamed, and took Harek's harp from him--for he carried it--and went forward boldly, singing the song of Gunnar in the snake pit. And it seemed to me that Harek would have chosen that song as fitting my case; for, putting Danes for snakes, I was in a close place enough. The warriors came out when they heard me; and I was well treated, and listened as I drank. Many things I learned."

Now I cannot believe that Alfred feared at all. He was surely but anxious, and took that feeling for fear. So think all his people.

"It seems that they thought I sang well," he went on; "so they took me to Guthrum. He indeed looked sharply at me once, and maybe twice; but I went on singing Harek's songs, and paid no heed to him. Presently he gave me a great horn of ale from his own table, and this gold bracelet that I wear also, and sent me away. Then I went about the camp and heard the talk. One man asked me if I had seen Alfred, and what he was like. 'Faith,' said I, 'men say I am like him.' Whereat they laughed long at me and at the king also. Then heard I the truth about my own looks for once. I had some trouble in getting away, but at last I seemed to wax hoarse, and so made as if I would go to Bridgwater, and left them, promising to come again. Ay, and I will keep my promise," he said; "but as Harek's heathen songs say, it is the sword's mass that I will sing to them."

Then his eyes glowed, and he was silent, and I wondered at the courage and resource in the slight figure that was before me.

"All goes well, and the plan is good," he went on directly. "They look for some easily-beaten attack from this side of the Parret, and at the first sign thereof will leave Edington height for the level ground below, as they did when Hubba came. Then when they turn, on Edington hill will be our levy suddenly--a levy of which they have not dreamed. And there will be the greatest fight that England has seen yet, and after that there will be a Saxon overlord of England against whom none will dare rise."

"May it be so, my king," I answered.

"It will be so," he said. "Here in this cottage have I had the word that tells me thereof; and you, Ranald, brought the sign that made the word sure to me."

I minded it, and I knew that for all my life my ways were bound to the service of Alfred the king; for my fate was linked with his, as it seemed, from my first coming.

It was not long now before the day came that will never be forgotten; for word was brought in from every quarter that thanes and freemen and churls alike would not be behind when Alfred gave the word, and he sent back to bid them meet him at Ecgbryht's Stone, beyond Selwood, on Whitsunday. There is a great and strong camp there on a rocky hill that looks out far and wide, near the two great roads, British and Roman, that cross in the vale beneath; and to that all were to gather, for there would the Golden Dragon be set up. Men call it White Sheet Castle.

On the day before I rode to Odda, who had already drawn his men to the Petherton ridge above Bridgwater, and told him what the king's word was. Then I went on up the long side of the Quantocks, and spoke in the Maytime woods with Thora, telling her--for she was a warrior's daughter, and was worthy of a warrior's love--that I must be at the king's side. And so she bade me fight bravely, speaking many noble and loving words to me, until I must go. Then I led her back to Osmund in his place among the rough huts within the wide circle of the camp ramparts, that now held but a few poor folk from the Parretside lands.

"King Alfred makes some new move," I said to him, "and it is possible that we may not meet again. I think that what is coming will end all the trouble between Saxon and Dane."

He shook his head.

"Some day it will end," he said, "but not in my time or yours--not until the Danes have grown to know that England is their home, and that they are English by birth and right of time-- maybe not till Denmark has ceased to send forth the sons for whom she has no place in her own borders."

Then I answered that perhaps he was right. I did not see into things as far as he, and I was a stranger in the land."

"But this at last will give a strong overlord to England," I said.

"Ay, for the time. So long as a strong king rules, there will be less trouble indeed; but if Alfred's sons are weak, it will begin afresh. England will no longer bear two kings; and while there is a Saxon kingdom alongside a Danish, there cannot be lasting peace."

Then I said:

"What of yourself? Shall you go back to Guthrum when this is over?"

"I cannot tell," he answered. "What my fate is I know not yet. What mean you to do if all goes well for Alfred? Shall you bide in England?"

We had walked apart now, and were looking over all the fair Quantock vale beneath us. I think there is no fairer lookout in all England: land and river and hills and sea, and beyond the sea the blue mountains of the Welsh coast--ever changing and ever beautiful under sun and cloud and flying shadows.

"I have found the fairest land under the northern sun," I said; "and I have found the best king, as I think. I shall bide here. One other thing I have found of which I hardly dare to think, so many are the chances of wartime. Yet, jarl, but for them I should not have met with Thora, though in my heart I believe that I should not have spoken to her yet."

"I would not have had it otherwise," he said, kindly taking my arm. "I have seen what was coming long before Etheldreda spoke. It has been good for Thora that she did so, whatever befalls."

Then we spoke of my promised place with the king, as if his victory were certain. Indeed, I believe that we both had no thought of its being otherwise.

"I do not know, however," said Osmund, "if your taking a Danish wife will be well received. It may be likely that Alfred will wish you to be bound to him by some tie of that nearness which shall be of his making."

I had not thought of that, but it was a thing that was common enough. Harald Fairhair was wont to give a rich wife to some chief whom he would keep at his side.

"If that is so, I shall go hence," I said. "There are things that come before friendship."

"Well," he answered, "we shall see. There is always a place for us both at Rolf's side in his new-won land."

"Yet I should be loth to leave Alfred," I said most truly. "I think that this is the only thing that would make me do so."

"Thora would not stand in your way to honour with him, nor would I," said Osmund.

"Honour with Alfred shall not stand in my way, rather," I answered. "But we speak of chances, as I think."

We said no more, and he bade me farewell.

I went back to Alfred somewhat sad, and yet with many thoughts that were good and full of hope; and soon I had little time to do aught but look on at the way in which the king's plans worked out most wonderfully.

On the eve of the great Whitsunday festival we set out through the fen paths southward to the hills and the first woodlands of Selwood Forest, and when the morning came we were far in its depths, passing eastward towards the place where we were to meet the levy.

Presently we turned aside to a little woodland chapel that had escaped the sight of the Danes, and from a hut beside it came out an old priest, white-bearded and bent with age and scanty fare. At first he feared that the heathen had found him at last; yet he looked bravely at us, catching up the crucifix that hung at his side and clasping it in both his hands as he stood in the open doorway of his church, as if to stay us from it.

Alfred rode forward to him when he saw his fear.

"Father, I am Alfred the king," he said. "Far have I ridden on this holy day. Now I would fain hear mass and have your blessing before we go on."

Thereat the old priest gave thanks openly to the King of kings, who had brought Alfred again into the land, and hastened to make ready. So that was the king's Whitsuntide mass, and we three heathen and our few men must bide outside while the others went into the holy place and returned with bright faces and happy; for this was a service to which we might not be admitted, though all knew that we would be Christians indeed ere long.

So at last we came to the ancient castle, and saw the valley to north and east beneath its height, bright everywhere with sparkling arms that gleamed from lane and field and forest glade, as all Wessex gathered to meet their king.

Then the Golden Dragon that we had lost and won was unfurled; and the war horns blew bravely enough to wake the mighty dead whose mounds were round about us; and soon the hillside was full of men who crowded upwards and filled the camp and ramparts and fosse, so that before sunset Alfred had a host that any king might be proud to call his own. Yet he would call it not Alfred's force, but England's.

Standing on the old ramparts, he spoke to them, while all the great gathering was silent. And the words he said sank into the heart of every man who heard, so that he felt as if on his arm alone it rested to free England, and that his arm could not fail. Not long did the king speak, but when he ended there rose a cheering that was good to hear, for it came from hearts that had been made strong to dare aught that might come.

After that he spoke to the thanes, giving each one his place, and telling them all that he had planned, so that each knew what was looked for from him. It seemed that he had forgotten nothing, and that the day must go as he said he thought it would.

Men slept on their arms that night, without watch fires, lest any prowling Danes should see that somewhat was on hand, although Guthrum had drawn to him every man from out of Wessex, as was said, and as seemed true. I have heard tales from some that in the night the warriors who lie resting in the mounds around their old stronghold came forth and wandered restless along the ramparts, longing to take their part again in the mighty struggle they knew was coming. I saw nothing, but Harek the scald says he saw.

Next day we marched towards our foes. Eighteen miles we went, and then came to the holy place Glastonbury, where the burnt ruins spoke again, as it were, to the warriors of wrong and cruelty to be avenged.

There we were, but eight miles from the foe, and that night we lay in a great meadow they called Iglea, deep down in the folds of the hills, where even so great a host might be hidden for many days if no chance betrayed them. Alfred took a few of us when night came, and climbed the steep tor above Glastonbury town. Thence we could see the long line of fires on Polden Hills that marked where the Danes slept, all unknowing that any host could be gathered in their rear.

In the grey of morning we set our ranks in order. I was with Alfred, with Ethered of Mercia and Ethelnoth, and more nobles whom I knew; and my few men were in the shield wall, among the best warriors of the Saxon levies. None grudged that honour to those who had made the point of the wedge that broke Hubba's ranks and won the Raven banner.

Now, in our Norse land there is ever sacrifice to the Asir when one leads a host to battle, that luck may be on the right side; and now I was to see a more wondrous thing than even that. I knew by this time the meaning of what I saw, and there crept into my heart a wish that I might take full part therein with Alfred, who had taught me.

When all the ranks were ordered, and the deep columns were drawn up on Iglea meadows in three sides of a square, there came a little train of robed monks, at whose head was Bishop Sigehelm of Sherborne, before whom went a tall gilded cross. Careworn and anxious looked the good fathers, for there was not one of them who had not a tale of Danish cruelty and destruction to tell, and more than one had hardly escaped with his life; but now their faces were brighter with new hope as they came into the open side of the armed square and waited for a moment.

Alfred and we stood before them, and the bishop raised his hand. At that we all knelt, with a strange clash and rattle of arms that went round the great host and ceased suddenly, so that the stillness was very great.

Then was only the voice of the bishop, who in a clear tone spoke the words of peace to those who should pass hence in the coming battle, that they might fight bravely, and even rejoice in death.

So he shrived the host, and at the end they said "Amen" in one voice.

Thereafter the bishop prayed to the Lord of hosts--not such a prayer as I had been wont to hear, but more wonderful, and with no boasting therein, nor, as it were, any hate of the foe, but rather the wish that the strife should make for peace, and even blessing to them.

Then he lifted his hand and blessed all the host as they bared their heads, and again the last word rolled deep and strong round the ranks, and that was all; then Alfred cried cheerily to his men, and we began our march that must needs end in battle.

There is a great road that climbs up the slope of the Polden Hills from Glastonbury and then runs along their top to Edington and beyond, and by this way we went, among pleasant woodlands. Guthrum's own place was on the spur of Edington, because thence one looks out on all the land that Alfred held, from the fort at Stane hill to Bridgwater and Combwich and the sea beyond. That was only eight miles from us, and was the point which we would win. Thence to Bridgwater is five miles, and the town was now held in force by the Danes; and where the road leaves the hills to cross the marsh to the bridge and town, two miles away, was a camp that guarded the causeway through the level.

We went quickly as a great host may, and Alfred had so ordered matters that even as we set out from Iglea, Odda and his force were moving in battle array from the Petherton heights on the Quantock side of the town, as if to attack it. That was what Guthrum had looked for since the time we had beaten Hubba, and the only attack which could have seemed possible in any way.

It is likely that he overrated the number which Odda had with him; for those who escaped us at Combwich had not been near enough to see from the far side of the river how small our force was, and would make much of those who had been able to overcome their mightiest chief. Moreover, since that time seven weeks had gone by, and the gathering of Devon might be greater yet. So it was, indeed; but Odda had not a thousand men. Perhaps, too, the Danes feared some sally from the fens; but however it was, they made not the mistake which destroyed Hubba by despising us rashly, for Guthrum drew his whole force together, and left the hills for a march towards the town which he heard was threatened.

So when we came to Edington, Guthrum's hill fort was empty, save for a camp guard to keep the country folk who lurked in wood and fen from pillaging it. These men fled, and we stood on the ridge without striking one blow; and King Alfred turned to us, and cried that surely his plan was working out well.

Then our host lined the ridge, and a mighty Saxon cheer from ten thousand throats went pealing across the valley below us, and they say that shout was heard even in Bridgwater. Guthrum heard it as he rode with his host across the long causeway, and his men heard it and halted, and saw in their rear the blaze of war gear that shone from their own lines, and knew that they were pent in between fens and hills, with an unknown force ready to fall on them.

Whereon a panic very nearly seized them. Hubba's end was fresh in their minds, and it needed all that Guthrum could say to prevent them making for the town. But he minded them of old victories, and bade them not fear to face the despised Saxons once again, and they rallied. But it was noon before he could lead them to attack us, and by that time he learned that Odda had halted above the town, and need not be feared. But by that time also every post of vantage along the hills was in our hands, and if Edington height was to be held by Danes again, it must be won by hard fighting. That is a thing that no Dane shrinks from, and now for Guthrum there was nought else to be done, for he was surrounded, as it were.

No man saw the whole of that fight, for it began at noon, as I have said, when Guthrum turned to find the hillward road blocked behind him. And from that time on it raged from spur to spur and point to point, as step by step the Danes won back to the hillsides. But the crest of the hill they never gained, save where for a time they might set foot and be driven headlong in turn by those who had given way before them at first. And so the fight swept on to the base of Edington hill and along its sides, for there Alfred had held his best men in reserve. Already the Danes had made for themselves some shallow lines of earthworks along the crest, and now these were manned against their own attack.

Men who looked on from afar tell strange tales of the shouts and cries that rang among the quiet Polden hills and woodlands that day for long hours. It was very still, as it chanced, and the noise of battle went far and wide from the place where Saxon and Dane fought their greatest fight for mastery.

Ever rode Alfred with the light of battle on his face, confident and joyous, among his men from post to post. Ever where the tide of battle seemed to set against us his arm brought victory again, until at last Guthrum drew his men together for one final attack that should end the day.

On Edington hillside he massed them, and steadily they came on under shield in a dense column to where, in their own camp, we waited under the Dragon banner. Half our men, the best spearmen of the force, were lying down resting, but along the little ridges of the earthworks the archers stood, each knowing that he fought under the eye of the king he loved.

"This is the end," said Alfred, as the Danes came on. "Be ready, spearmen, when I give the word."

And they lay clutching their weapons, with their eyes fixed on him as he stood on the hilltop, surrounded by his thanes, gazing on the last assault of the Danes, whose archers from the wings were already at work, so that the men of the shield wall closed in around him.

I think that the Danes had no knowledge of what force was hidden by the hill brow. For when they were within half arrow shot, and Alfred gave the word, and the long ranks of spearmen leaped from the ground and closed up for their charge, a waver went along the shielded line, and they almost halted, though it passed, and they came on even more swiftly.

Then Alfred lifted his sword and shouted, and, with that awful roar that I had heard before on the Combwich meadows, over the hill crest and down upon the Danes the spearmen rushed. The lines met with a mighty crash of steel on steel, and while one might count two score they swayed in deadly hand-to-hand strife. Then Guthrum's men gave back one pace, and howled, and won their place again, and again lost it.

Then forward went Alfred and his shield wall, and I was on one side of him and Ethered of Mercia on the other, while after him came Heregar, bearing the banner. The Danes in the centre closed up as they saw us come, and there were shouts in which Guthrum's name was plain to be heard, and I saw him across a four-deep rank of his men.

Straight for him went Alfred, and the Danish line grew thin before us. But as their king went forward our Saxons cheered again and pressed their attack home, and right and left the Danish line fell back and broke. At that a wild shout and charge with levelled spears swept them down the hillside in full rout, and the end had come. His courtmen closed round Guthrum and bore him from before us, and the full tide of pursuit swept him away before we reached him.

Alfred stayed his horse and let the men go on. His face was good to see as he glanced round at the hills to our right; but when it fell on the slain, who lay thickly where the lines had met, he bared his head and looked silently on them for a space, while his lips moved as if he prayed.

Then he said:

"These have given their lives not in vain, for they have helped to bring peace, and have died to set an English king over the English land."

He put on his crown-circled helm again, and as he did so, among the fallen there was a stir and movement, and the wounded rose up on arms and knees and turned on their sides, and raised their hands, waving broken weapons, and crying in a strange, wearied voice that yet had a ring of victory in it:

"Waeshael to Alfred the king!"

For the silence that had fallen, and the lessening shouts of the pursuers, told them that they had won, and they were content.

Thereat Alfred flushed red, and I think that he almost wept, for he turned from us. And then he spoke to the men who yet stood round him, and said:

"Let every man who has any knowledge of care for the wounded, or who has known a wound of his own and the way it was cared for, go among these brave ones and help them."

Nor would he leave the place till he saw men going up and down among the hurt, tending them as well as they could; and he was the more content when he saw Bishop Sigehelm and many other clergy come on the field from the rear, where he had bidden them stay. The bishop had mail under his robes, having been eager to join in the fight, as would Eahlstan, his great forerunner, have certainly joined; but Alfred would not suffer him to do so.

Once more Guthrum tried to rally his men, when the flight bore him to his camp at the hill foot, on the way across the fens to the town. There was a sharp fight there, and Ethelnoth was wounded as he led on his men; and thence the Danes fled to Bridgwater, making no more delay. So close on them were our men that Guthrum's housecarls closed the gates after their king on many of their comrades, who fell under the Saxon spear in sight of safety. Nor did we give them time to drive in the cattle that were gathered from all the countryside to the meadows round the place.

Then came Thord to me and put me in mind of somewhat.

"Now is our work to be done, king. These Danes will take Hubba's ships and be gone down the river next. We must stop them in some way, for the king's plan is to starve them out, as it seems."

We had left the king at that time, for we would not suffer him to join in pursuit, which has its dangers, if men turn desperate and make a stand, as many did, dying like brave warriors that they were. So I rode on quickly with my followers, and came to the river bank below the bridge. The Danes were swarming on the ramparts of the fortress like angry bees, and in the ships, which lay beneath the walls, men were busy, even as Thord had guessed they would be, making ready to sail when tide served. We could not reach them by any means, for every boat had been taken from this side long ago, when the first news of defeat was brought back by flying horsemen.

Then Thord's face glowered under his helm, and he pointed to the ship that was farthest from the bridge, and therefore likely to be the first to start away when the tide was full. It was my own ship, which they had got afloat.

"Thor's hammer smite them!" he growled; "they have launched the old keel without finishing her painting--just as I left her. How are we to stay their going off with her?"

"Is there a chain cable anywhere?" I asked.

"Not one in the place," he said; "and if we did get one across the river, we should have to fight to keep the far end of it."

The tide was rising fast, and I thought we should surely lose every ship, while Guthrum and his chiefs would escape us at the same time. One might line the banks with archers, certainly, but that would not stay the going. Evening was closing in, moreover. By midnight they would be gone, and I was in a difficulty out of which I could not see my way.

Suddenly Thord smote his hands together, and his face grew brighter.

"I have it," he cried. "There is an old vessel that lies in a creek a mile down the river. A great buss [lxvii] she is, and worth nothing; but she will float, and maybe will be afloat now. If we can sink her across the channel in a place that I know, not one of these ships will get away till she is raised."

Then I called every man to me whom I could see, and we went quickly to the place where this buss was, and she was just afloat. Thord knew where her tackle was kept, and he had the oars out--what there were of them at least, for they were old and rotten enough. Then we had to shove her off and get her boat into the water, and the vessel itself floated up on the tide towards the narrow place where she might best be sunk to block the channel against ships that came from the town.

We had not gone far when there came a sound at which I started, for it was nothing more or less than the quick beat of oars coming down the river against the tide. Thord and I and eight men of my own crew were in the buss, while I had maybe thirty men ashore who were keeping pace with us along the bank. The rest of my own men were with these, and one shouted that he could see the ship, and that it was our own, crammed with men too.

Now at first it seemed as if the only thing for us to do was to go ashore in the boat as quickly as we could and get away; but Thord cried to me:

"Then will the Danes take our ship to sea, and we have lost her for good. It should not be said of us that we let her go without a blow struck to save her."

"Sink this hulk straightway, then," I said, falling to work, with the axe I had in thy hand, on the lowest strakes. My men leaped to work as well, and in two minutes the seams began to gape, and then was a rush of water from broken planking that sent us over the side and into the boat in hot haste.

Then we pulled for shore, towing the bows of the fast-sinking buss with us till they grounded in the mud, and even as her stern swung with the tide across the channel she lurched and sank.

"We should have bided in her and fought," growled Thord. "Now in five minutes we shall see the bottom ripped out of our own ship by our own deed."

But a foot of the bows and the mast of the buss stood out of the water, and I thought the Danes would see these marks.

Even as we gained the shore our dragon stem swept round the bend that had hidden us, and came on swiftly. Then the Danes saw us, and those on the fore deck shouted, and the oars plashed wildly, and many on the side next to us stopped altogether; and at the same time the steersman saw the stem of the wreck, and, as I think, lost his head between fear of it and the sudden appearance of the foe whom he thought he had escaped. The larboard oars were going yet, and the starboard had almost stopped. He paid no heed to it, and the ship swung over. Then the tide caught her bows, and in a moment she ran hard and fast on our bank, and the men in her fell right and left with the shock.

I had seen what was coming, and so had Thord, and we ran our best to meet her as she struck. The tide was a good one, and she came well on the hard bank, and there was no need to tell my men what to do. Before the Danes knew what had happened we were climbing over the bows on board, and the Danes aft were leaping into the river to get away from us.

Some few tried to fight; but there must have been two hundred men packed along the gangways, and they could do nothing. They threw themselves into the water like the rats that had left the old buss even now, and we slew many, and the good ship was our own again. Some of the Danes got ashore on the far bank, some were met by our Saxons on this side, and but few got back to Bridgwater, for the river had most of them.

Another ship was coming at this time, but those in her heard the shouting and the cries; and it would seem that their hearts failed them, for they went back before we could see more than the tall mast above the banks from our decks.

Then we thought we might rest, for we were wearied out; but Thord would not suffer us to do so till he had got the ship carefully below the wreck, so that she was free. Had we waited for the next tide we could not have done it, as it turned out; for the rise of flood shortened quickly to the neap tides, and a bank of mud grew round the sunken hull, making the channel impassable altogether for the time, and so the last way of escape for Guthrum and his men was barred.

So I thought we had done well, and left Thord and my men to guard the ship and take her back to Combwich, where she would lie safely in the creek, while I rode to Alfred, almost sleeping on my wearied horse as I went.

There were two wrecks in that place in the morning; for they brought down one of Hubba's ships in the dark on the next tide, and she ran on the sunken stem of the buss, and went down almost at once. After that no more attempt was made to fly by water.

Then began a siege that lasted for a fortnight, without anything happening that is worth telling; for the fear of Alfred was on the Danes, and they had not heart so much as to make one sally from the gates.

Chapter XIII. The Greatest Victory.

Now in a few days it was plain that Alfred held the Danes in the hollow of his hand as it were, and could do what he would with them. At first we looked for messengers from the place, to treat with him for peace; but none came. From the town at times we could hear shoutings and the noise of men who quarrelled, as if there were divided counsels among them that led to blows. They were very short of food also, because all their stores of cattle were left outside the walls, as I have said, so that we fared the better for their plundering while we waited.

At the end of the first week, therefore, Alfred sent a message under flag of truce, and told the chiefs that he was willing to hear what they would say; and next day Guthrum asked that some chiefs might come and speak with him. But Alfred would not trust the Danes enough to send any of his nobles into the town, and bade Guthrum come out to the camp and say what he had to say. But he would not. Then one day, when Alfred held counsel as to what was best to be done to ensure lasting peace, I said that I thought Jarl Osmund might be of use, for he could go between the two camps in safety.

That seemed good to the king, and Heregar and I rode to find him, crossing the tidal ford at Combwich, where we heard from village folk who had returned that the Danish lord bided in Heregar's house beyond the fort.

There I thought I should find Thora, and we went quickly. The place looked very deserted, and when we came to the courtyard gates it seemed more so, for the Maytime had sprinkled the gay-patterned paving of grey and white shore pebbles with blades of grass and weeds that sprang up between them everywhere for want of tendance.

Only the Lady Alswythe and a few of her servants were there now, for the Lady Etheldreda had taken Thora with her to Taunton when she left the hills. It had not been so safe here, though there was little plunder to bring the Danes to the place now. So I need not say that I was grievously disappointed, though in the dismantled hall sat Osmund, listlessly shaping a bow stave, and waiting for what turn of fortune should take him next.

Very glad, as one might think, were both the lady and the jarl for our coming, and we had to tell them all the tale of the working of Alfred's plan, and of the great fight. And when that was heard, we told the jarl of Alfred's wish to treat with Guthrum and the other chiefs through him.

That Osmund would gladly do; indeed, he said that, in hopes of being thus useful, he had stayed so near at hand.

So he and the thane talked long of the matter--for Alfred had sent messages--while I spoke with the lady, of Thora mostly.

It did not seem to me that I had any part in the king's business with the Danes, and so presently I thought that I could do no better than ride to Taunton to see Thora, who I feared might be in trouble or doubt as to my safety.

So I rode there with Kolgrim. At that time the scald was laid up with a wound in the camp, and the king seemed to miss his presence, and to care for his welfare as if he were his brother; but, indeed, he made every man with whom he had to do feel as if his king were his best friend.

There is not much need for me to tell what manner of welcome I had at Taunton from Thora. As for Etheldreda, she would have me tell her everything, and I sat with those two, until night came and rest, talking of all the time past. But of the time to come Thora said nothing, and once or twice when Etheldreda left us and we were alone for a little while, so that I could try to plan out somewhat, she would but turn the talk again.

In the morning I found out how this was. She had gathered from Osmund somewhat of his thoughts about what Alfred's plan for me might be, and was unhappy therefore, not wishing to stand in my way to honour with the king. So she told me when I pressed her a little to speak of what I would do; and when I said that there should be nothing that I would let stand between us, she was the more troubled yet.

So at last I went and found Etheldreda, and prayed her to come and speak with Thora.

"Falling out already?" she said, laughing.

"Not so, but a greater trouble than that," I said, "one that will need your help before it is mended."

"Ay, I suppose you could patch up a quarrel for yourselves," she said. "What is this mighty trouble?"

So she came and sat by Thora, taking her hand and kissing her, and we told her what Osmund's thoughts were.

"There is such enmity between Saxon and Dane," Thora said, "that it is not likely that the king will trust one who will wed one of his foe's daughters."

It was plain that Etheldreda thought the same; but she cheered us both, saying that she would do all that she could to help us, and that Odda would not be behind in the matter. After all, if we were to wait for a while, things might be very different after a little time of peace. And so we were content.

So I went back to Alfred next day, and when he heard where I had been he smiled a little, and said:

"One thing I must tell you, my Norseman, and that is that our thanes who know little of you will be jealous that you should have much dealing with any Dane as yet."

Which made me the more uneasy; for though I might think that the king, at all events, was not displeased with me, others, and the wishes of others, might be too strong for him to go against.

But my affairs are little things compared with what was on hand at this time, and on the same day Alfred spoke to me about somewhat that he would have me do for him.

In the town the Danes were in the greatest straits by this time, for by no means could they get stores of any sort to them, so close was the watch round the place. Osmund had been in and out once or twice, and Guthrum had received him well enough, and it was thought that there would be no long delay now before the siege was at an end by the submission of the Danes to any terms they might gain, and the more so that an assault on the fortress would surely have been successful, ending in the fall of all its defenders.

But Alfred was most willing to be merciful, and he had bidden Osmund tell Guthrum and his chiefs that if he might name twelve hostages for himself the rest should go free, while Guthrum should hold the East Anglian kingdom for him as under-king.

But this was what Alfred would have me do.

"One other thing there is," he said. "If there is to be any brotherhood between us, it must be as between Christians. The ways of persecution must be forgotten and that cannot come to pass until the chiefs at least have accepted the faith."

"It is strange to me, my king," I said, "that Guthrum, who has been in England for ten years, is not Christian by this time."

"Ay, but his hosts are heathen," the king answered. "Now I think I can speak to you as if no longer a heathen at least?"

"As a Christian, my king," I answered.

"Well, then," he said, smiling on me, "go and speak to Guthrum and tell him what I have said. I think that he will listen to you better than if I sent a priest or even Bishop Sigehelm. Warrior may speak to warrior plainly."

Now this was a hard thing for me to do, as it seemed. Maybe it was the hardest thing he could have asked me. But it was in my mind that I could not but go to Guthrum and give the message, else would I seem to deny the faith that I loved. Alfred saw at once that I was troubled in some way, and I believe that he knew well what the seeming doubt was.

"Once you brought a token of good to me," he said. "Now that was all unknowing. Go now and take a message of good to Guthrum openly, and have no fear."

"What shall I say?"

"Mind not that at all," he answered; "what is needed will come to you."

So I said that I would go if Harek might come with me, for his words were ever ready. But Alfred would not suffer that. I must go without help from a scald, taking only my own words; and at last I consented, though indeed my only fear was that I might not succeed by reason of my slowness of speech.

Then I went to Osmund, and told him that I was to go into the town with him next day, for that is how Alfred planned for me; and I told him also what my part in the business was to be. Whereon he surprised me.

"I do not know that your errand is so hopeless as you seem to think," he said. "Guthrum has harmed no Christians in East Anglia since he was king there."

"Well," I answered, "I hope it may be easy, though I doubt it."

I would not say more then, but, being anxious, went and spoke long with Harek. The brave scald's wounds were deep, though he had said little of them. Some say that he saved the life of Ethelnoth at the time when that ealdorman was struck down, and that also is Ethelnoth's story; though the scald says that if so it was by accident, and less worth speaking of than many braver deeds that were wrought and went untold that day.

"Here have I been in England but six months or so, and I have more to sing of than ever I learned with Harald Fairhair," he said one day, as he made songs on his bed while his wounds were healing.

And he spoke the truth. Never was a winter so full of deeds wrought by a king and a valiant people that were worth a scald's remembrance.

Now Osmund had a last message from Alfred that day, and in the morning we went together to the bridge. There Guthrum's own courtmen met us, and they took us into the fortress, beyond which lies the town, so that we saw little of what straits the host might be in by this time. In the fortress itself all seemed in order at least; and there was a guard set at the door of the well-built hut where the Danish king was, as if some state were yet kept up.

There Guthrum welcomed us, and with him were many chiefs, on whose faces was the same care-worn look that Osmund had borne when I saw him at Exeter before Alfred.

"Two messages come to you today," Osmund said; "one by my mouth, and the other by that of King Ranald Vemundsson, who is with me. I think you may hear both, and answer them both favourably."

Guthrum made no reply, but took his seat at the upper end of the one room the hut had; and all the chiefs sat also, leaving us messengers standing.

Then said Osmund:

"I think it right that I should stand in the presence of my king, but the son of King Vemund should not do so in any less presence than that of his overlord."

Thereat Guthrum smiled a little.

"I have heard that Harald of Norway came to blows with his brother kings because they would not stand before him, and that others have left that kingdom because they did not choose to do so. Sit down, King Ranald. Your father's name was well known to all of us in the old days. I am glad to see his son, though maybe I should not say so."

"We would rather that he were on our side," said one of the other chiefs.

Then they set places for both of us, and we waited for Guthrum's word.

"Well," he said, wearily enough, "let us hear what King Alfred says."

"Few are his words," said Osmund:

"'Let Guthrum suffer me to choose any hostages that I will for myself, let him swear to keep the peace hereafter as my under-king beyond Thames, doing homage to me, and he shall go hence with his host in honour.' There is also the message of Ranald to add hereto."

Now I thought that the faces of the chiefs showed that they thought these terms very light;

but they said nothing as yet.

Guthrum turned to me.

"Well, King Ranald?"

"Alfred the king bids me say that he would fain treat with you hereafter as a brother altogether. And that can only be if the great trouble between Dane and Saxon is removed--that is, if Guthrum becomes a Christian."

Now I expected some outburst of scorn and wrath on this, but instead of that a silence fell, in which the chiefs looked at one another; and Guthrum gazed at me steadfastly, so that I felt my face growing hot under his eyes, because I knew I must say more, and that of myself and my own wishes most likely.

Then Guthrum said slowly:

"Why has he not sent some priest to say this?"

"Because he thought that a warrior would listen best to a brother warrior," I answered.

"Ay, that is true," said the king. "Are you a Christian, therefore?"

"I am as yet unbaptized," I said. "I have taken the prime signing on me, as have many others; but I shall certainly seek baptism shortly."

"You came here as a heathen, then?"

"As a heathen altogether, except that I had no hatred of Christians," I answered, not quite seeing what the king would know.

"What turned your mind so far from the old gods that you should be a fit messenger on such a matter to us?"

"I have learned from Alfred and Neot," I answered, "and I know that I have found what is true."

Then Guthrum turned to Osmund.

"What say you, jarl? you have been with Alfred also."

"When Ranald is baptized, I shall be so with him," the jarl answered simply.

And that was the first word thereof that I had heard from him.

Then an older chief spoke sharply to us.

"What profit do you look to make thereout--either of you?"

"Certainty of better things both in this life and in that to come," I answered.

"Ay, so they always say," the chief growled; "but what place with Alfred in return?"

"It is likely that I shall gain no place with him," I said. "Jarl Osmund knows that I do not count on that."

"Ay," said Osmund, "I know it. Nor will any man think that I seek honour at Alfred's hands."

Then Guthrum rose up, and spoke gravely and yet very determinedly, as if this was no new matter to him.

"Here, chiefs, are two good and tried warriors who willingly choose Alfred's faith. You and I have heard thereof since we were in England; and many a man have we seen die, since we have been here, because he would not give it up. I mind me of Edmund, the martyred king, whom Ingvar, our great chief, slew, and of Humbert the bishop, and many more lesser folk. Tell me truly how much you have thought of the Asir in these last years?"

But none answered. It was with them as with me: the Asir were not of England.

"One thing," said Guthrum, "has gone against our taking up the English faith--we have thought the words of peace have made men cowardly. Now we know that is not so. Here is one who withstood Hubba, and round the walls watch Christian men who have beaten us sturdily."

Then he stayed his words for a little, and his voice sank, and he looked round and added:

"Moreover, the words of the new faith are good. I will accept King Alfred's brotherhood altogether."

Then one or two more of the younger chiefs spoke, and said that they would do so also; but again the elder warrior spoke fiercely.

"Is this forced on us as part of the peace making?"

"It is not," I answered. "It is, as I have said, the wish for brotherhood altogether."

Then said Guthrum:

"That is enough. I do not think that we need be ashamed to be conquered altogether by King Alfred."

"One more word," said the old chief. "Are we to have no hostages?"

"There can be no exchange of hostages," said Osmund.

"Things are all on the side of the Saxon," he growled.

"Ay, they are, in more ways than that," said Guthrum. "We have no power to say a word. It is in my mind that we could not have looked for such mildness at the king's hands. For there is no denying that we are at his mercy.

"What say you, as a stranger, Ranald?"

"I have known the ways of Harald of Norway," I answered. "I think that he would not have left a man of this host alive."

Whereon the old warrior laughed shortly, and was silent while Guthrum bade us go back to Alfred and thank the king for his word, saying that an answer should be given as soon as the word of the host had been taken in open Thing.

So Alfred won Guthrum to the faith, and greatly did he rejoice when he heard what the Danish king had said. I think he was more glad yet when he knew that Osmund would become Christian also, and he urged us both to be baptized at once.

"Let us be so with Guthrum," I asked.

"That will be fitting," he answered, "for I think you have won him over."

But I hold that Guthrum and more of his chiefs had been won by the deaths of those martyrs of whom he spoke long before the choice was set before him. One cannot tell how this was wrought in the mind of the Danes altogether by the hand of God. Some will ever say, no doubt, that they took the Cross on them by necessity; but I know that it was not so. Nor have their lives since that time given any reason for the thought.

Then Alfred asked the name of that old warrior who withstood us, and Osmund told him.

"I will have that chief as a hostage," the king said, "for I think that he is worth taming."

"I think that King Alfred's hostages are not in any way to be pitied," Osmund said.

"Save that they are kept from home and friends, I would have them as happy as may be," the king answered; "but I would have none presume on what mercy came to you, Jarl Osmund, for the sake of the Christmastide message."

"I think that none will do so," Osmund said. "There is full knowledge among my kin that you showed mercy when justice was about to be done, and well they know that your kindness was not weakness. It is likely that the mercy shown here also will do more for peace than would even destruction of your enemies."

So it seemed at last, for on the fourteenth day of the siege the Danes accepted the king's terms with one consent. And more than that, Guthrum and thirty of his chiefs asked that they might be baptized; which was a wonder to all of our host.

Now I have said nothing about the life in the great camp before Bridgwater, for it had nothing of much note to me, though it was pleasant enough. I think there was some jealousy of me among the younger thanes at one time; but it passed because I would not notice it, and also because I took no sort of authority on me, being only the king's guest and warrior as yet. But I did find a few young thanes of Odda's following who knew somewhat of the sea, and I was wont to talk with them often of the ships and the like, until I knew they would be glad to take to the viking's path with me in the king's ships, bringing their men with them. And often Alfred spoke with me of the matter, until I was sure that he would have me stay.

It was but a few days after the peace had been made when Alfred went to a great house he had at Aller, which lies right amidst the marshes south of Athelney. We had saved that house and the church by our constant annoyance of the Danes, with many another house and village along the fen to which they dared not come for fear of us at last. Guthrum was to come to him there, and I think that he chose the place because there at least was nought to bring thoughts of defeat to the Danes, and there they could be treated as guests, apart from the great camp and fortress. Great were the preparations there for the high festival that should be when Alfred himself should take Guthrum to the font.

Then came Neot on foot, with Guerir his fellow hermit, from Cornwall, to be present; and Harek and I rejoiced as much as the king that he had come.

"I think I must answer for you two at the font," he said.

"For Kolgrim also, I pray you, Father Neot," said I; "for he will be baptized with us."

"Ay, for honest Kolgrim also," he answered; "but what of old Thord, my reprover?"

"He will have nought to do with the new faith," I said. "But at least he does not blame us for leaving the old gods. He says he is too old to learn what we younger men think good."

"I will seek him and speak with him again," Neot said. "I think I owe him somewhat."

Then we thanked the holy man for the honour that he was showing us; but he put thanks aside, saying that we were his sons in the truth, and that the honour was his rather.

Now in the seven weeks that we waited for Guthrum at Aller, while the priests whom Alfred sent taught him and his chiefs what they should know rightly before baptism, Osmund and I were wont to go to Taunton, across the well-known fens, and bide for days at a time in Odda's house there, and we told Thora for what we waited.

She had come to England, when she was quite a child, with the first women who came into East Anglia, and already she knew much of Christianity from the Anglian thralls who had tended her. And when she had heard more of late from Etheldreda and Alswythe, she had longed to be of the same faith as these friends of hers, and now rejoiced openly.

"Ranald," she said, "I had not dared to speak of this to my father, but I was wont to fear the old gods terribly. They have no place for a maiden in their wild heaven. There are many more Danish ladies who long for this change, even as I have longed. Yet I still fear the wrath of Odin for you and my father."

"The old gods are nought--they have no power at all," I said, bravely enough; though even yet I had a little fear in thus defying them, as it seemed.

"Then I will dread them no more," she answered. "Nor do I think that you need fear them."

So I comforted her, and bade her ask more of Etheldreda, who would gladly teach her; and the matter passed by in gladness, as a trouble put away, for she and I were at one in this. I will say that I had half feared that she whom I loved would have been angry with me.

Now on that night Osmund and I and Harek would ride to Heregar's house over the shoulder of the Quantocks, with some message we had to take to him from Alfred; and we went without any attendants, for the twelve miles or so would have no risk to any one, and the summer evening was long and bright.

Yet we were later in starting away than we should have been, and so when we were among the wilder folds of the hills, where the bare summits rise from wooded slopes and combes, we were overtaken by a heavy thunderstorm that came up swiftly from the west behind us, darkening the last sunset light with black clouds through which the lightning flickered ceaselessly.

We rode on steadily, looking for some place of shelter; but it grew very dark, and the narrow track was rough, and full of loose stones that made the going slow. Presently the clouds settled down on the hill crest and wrapped us round, and the storm broke afresh on us, with thunder that came even as the darkness was changed to blue brightness with the lightning flashes that played around us almost unceasing. There was no rain yet and no wind, and the heat grew with the storm.

Soon the nearness of the flashes scared our horses, and we had to dismount and lead them, and in the darkness we lost the little track among the heavy heather. And then there seemed to me to be a new sound rising among the thunder, and I called to Harek, bidding him hearken.

It came from seaward, and swelled up louder and louder and nearer, until it passed over our heads--the yelp and bay of Odin's wild hounds, and the trample and scream of his horses and their dead riders. A great fear fell on me, so that the cold sweat stood on my forehead, while the hunt seemed everywhere above us for a moment, and then passed inland among the thunder that hardly drowned its noises.

Then Osmund the jarl cried out:

"That was Odin's hunt. I have heard it before, and ill came thereof. He hunts us who forsake him."

And out of the darkness Harek answered, without one shake in his brave voice:

"Odin's hunt in truth it was, and the ill comes to Odin, who must leave this land before the might of the Cross. We who bear the sign of might he cannot touch."

Then I remembered myself, and the fear passed from me, and I was ashamed. I had no doubt now that there was need for Odin's wrath, seeing that he was surely defeated. And Osmund was silent also, thinking doubtless the same things; for he had taken on him the prime signing long ago, and had forgotten it maybe.

Then we went on, and the storm grew wilder. Harek sang now, but what the words were I cannot tell. I think they were some that he had learned from Alfred.

Now we began to go down the southern slope of the highest neck of the hill, as it seemed, though we could not rightly say where we were, and in a little silence that came between the thunderclaps I heard the rattle of hoofs as of another rider coming after us, going faster than we dared.

"Here is one who knows the hill well," I said; "maybe he will guide us."

And then the lightning showed the horseman close to us. He reined up, and cried in a great voice:

"Ho, strangers! are you wandering here?"

"Ay; we are lost till the storm passes. Can you guide us to shelter before the rain comes?" I said.

"Whence come you?" he asked.

"We are Alfred's men from Taunton--going to the thane's house at Cannington."

"Ay, is that so? Then I will guide you. Follow," he said, and he rode on.

One could see him plainly when the lightning came, and it showed a tall man, grey bearded, and clad in a long hooded horseman's cloak, under which gleamed golden-shining mail. Well mounted on a great horse he was also, and its sides were white with foam on the dark skin, as though he had ridden hard.

We mounted and went after him, with the lightning playing round us and glancing from the mail of our leader as his arm threw the cloak back over his shoulder from time to time. He led us along the hill crest northward, crossing the places where the fire beacons had been; and we wondered whither he was taking us, for shelter here was none. And now the storm grew wilder, with the wind and chill of coming rain.

Then he turned downhill, riding fast until we came to a place where rocks lay loose and scattered everywhere, and our horses stumbled among them. There he reined up suddenly, holding up his hand, and shouting through the uproar of wind and thunder:

"Hold, for your lives! Hearken!"

We stayed motionless, listening, and again we heard the cry and clang of Odin's hunt, coming now from inland over us, and I made the sign of the Cross on my breast, in fear thereof.

"Ho for Odin's hunt!" the strange man cried, in his mighty voice. "Hear it, Alfred's men, for you shall join it and ride the wind with him if you defy him."

"We fear him not," said Harek; "he has no power over us."

"Has he not?" the man roared, facing full upon us; and as he did so the lightning glared on him, and I saw that his drawn sword was aloft, and that from its point glowed a blue flame, and that blue flames also seemed to start from his horse's ears. One-eyed the man was also, and he glowered on us under shaggy eyebrows.

Harek saw also, and he raised his hand towards the man and signed the holy sign, crying:

"Speak! who are you?"

Thereat the man gave a hoarse roar as of rage, and his horse reared, trampling wildly on the loose rocks, and, lo, he was gone from before our eyes as if he had never been, while the thunder crashed above us and below us everywhere!

"Odin! the Cross has conquered!" Harek cried again, in a voice that was full of triumph; and the blood rushed wildly through me at the thought of what I had seen.

Then Harek's horse shifted, and his hoof struck a great stone that rolled as if going far down the hill, and then stopped, and maybe after one could count five came a crash and rattle underneath us that died away far down somewhere in the bowels of the hill. And at that Osmund shouted suddenly:

"Back to the hill; we are on the brink of the old mine shaft! Back, and stay not!"

Nor did we wait, but we won back to the higher ground before we drew rein.

"We have met with Odin himself," Osmund said when we stopped and the thunder let him speak.

"Ay, and have driven him hellwards by the might of the holy sign," said Harek. "Nearly had he lured us to death, unbaptized as we are, in that place."

"Come," said Osmund; "I know where we are now. We are well-nigh under the great fort, and there is a farm near at hand."

We found that soon and the rain came, and the storm spent its fury and passed as we sat under cover in the stables waiting. Then came the moonlight and calm, and the sweetness of rain-soaked earth and flowers refreshed, and we went on our way wondering, and came to the thane's with the first daylight. And I thought that our faces were pale and marked with the terror of the things through which we had gone, and maybe also with a new light of victory [lxvii].

Chapter XIV. King Alfred's Will.

When we came back to Aller, the first thing that I did was to tell Neot of our meeting with Odin while his wild hunt went on through the tempest, telling him how that I had feared unwisely, and also of Harek's brave withstanding of the danger.

"It is said that our forefathers met Odin in like wise in the days of the first christening of our race," he said. "I do not know what to make thereof, seeing that I hold Odin as nought; but I think this, that in some way Satan tried to destroy you before you were baptized. Wherefore, whether Odin or mortal man drew you to that place, I have no doubt what power saved you."

But Sigehelm thought that we had met with Satan himself in the shape of the old god, and so also thought Guerir the hermit, who told strange tales of like appearings among the Welsh hills where he was born.

As for Alfred the king, he marvelled, and said even as Neot. But he added this:

"I know the mine shaft well, and it is in my mind that some day Odin's bones will be found at the bottom thereof. Nevertheless there is more than mortal in what has happened to you by way of trial."

Now came the time when Guthrum and his thirty comrades should seek the king, and I have no words to tell of that time when in the peaceful church we heathen stood white-robed and unarmed altogether at the font, while Sigehelm, with a wonderful gathering of priests, enlisted us as warriors of the Cross. It was, as all men think, the most mighty victory that Alfred had ever gained.

At that time he chose Guthrum as his own son in the faith, and named him Athelstan [lxviii], as the first and most noble stone of the new building up of the church among the Danes. Neot would not have our names changed, for he said we had wronged the faith in them not at all. Odda stood for Osmund, as Neot for us.

After that was joyous feasting, and the loosing of the chrism bands at Alfred's royal town of Wedmore, whither we went in bright procession through the long summer day. Four days we bided there, till we knew that the great Danish host was on its march homewards, and then Guthrum and his comrades must join it. But before he went he accepted from Alfred the gifts that an under-king should take from his overlord, and they were most splendid. All men knew by those tokens given and taken that Alfred was king indeed, and that Guthrum did but hold place by his sufferance. Those two parted in wondrous friendship with the new bond of the faith woven round them, and the host passed from Wessex and was gone.

Yet, as ever, many a long year must pass by before the track of the Danes should be blotted out from the fair land they had laid waste. Everywhere was work to hand on burnt hall and homestead, ruined church, and wasted monastery. There was nought that men grieved over more than the burning of King Ine's church at Glastonbury, for that had been the pride of all the land. Once, after the Chippenham flight, the monks had dared to go out in sad procession to meet the fierce raiders at the long dike that bars the way to Avalon, and for that time they had won safety for the place--maybe by the loss of their treasures given as ransom, or, as some say, by the power of fearless and unarmed men; for there were men in the Danish host whose minds were noble, and might well be touched thereby. But Hubba's men could not be withheld after they had lost their mighty leader, and the place must feel their fury of revenge.

Now after the host was gone we went back to Taunton, and there Alfred called together his Witan, that he might set all things in order with their help; and at that time, before the levies were dismissed, he bade me seek out such men as would take to the ships as his paid seamen. Therein I had no hard task, for from the ruined coast towns came seafarers, homeless and lonely, asking nought better than to find a place in the king's fleet, and first of all were the Parret-mouth men and my fisher of Wareham. Presently, with one consent, the Witan made me leader of the king's Wessex sea levies, offering me the rank and fee of an English ealdorman, with power to demand help in the king's name from all sea-coast sheriffs and port reeves in whatever was needed for the ships, being answerable to the throne only for what I should do. And that I accepted willingly for love of Alfred, who was my friend, and for the sake of comradeship with those valiant men who had fought beside me when Hubba fell, and at Edington.

Then must I set myself to my new charge, having nought to do with all the inland work that was before the king; and when the next day's business was over, I went to tell him of this wish of mine, and of some other matters that were on my mind whereof one may easily guess.

Alfred sat in his private chamber in the great house that King Ine built, and on the table before him were a great ink horn and other writing gear, and beside him sat on a low stool his chaplain, reading to him out of a great book while the king wrote. The rough horn cage wherein was a candle, that he had planned in wind-swept Athelney, stood close at hand, against the time of dusk that was near. Ever was Alfred planning things like this, even in his greatest troubles; and therein he was wise, for it is not good to keep the mind full of heavy things alone. Moreover, as we wondered at his skilful devices in these little things, we took heart from his cheerful pleasure in them.

When the chamberlain brought me in, the great book was put aside, and the pen set down, and the king looked up at me with his bright smile.

"Welcome, my ship thane," he said. "Come and sit here beside me. I have somewhat to read to you."

So I sat down wondering, and he turned back to some place in his writing, and took the little knife that lay by him--for he had lost his jewelled book staff in Athelney--and running its point along the words, read to me from the writings of some old Roman what he had been busy putting into good Saxon:

"Now when the Roman folk would make a fleet hastily, and had no rowers, nor time to train them rightly, they built stages like to the oar benches of a ship in a certain lake, and so taught the men the swing and catch of the long oars."

"Will not that plan serve us, Ranald?" he said.

"Ay, lord," I answered, laughing. "In good truth, if a man can learn to keep time, and swing rightly, and back water, and the like, on such a staging, it is somewhat. But it will be hard work pulling against dead water from a stage that moves not. Nor will there be the roll and plunge of waves that must be met."

"Nor the sore sickness whereof Odda speaks," Alfred said, with his eyes twinkling. "But I think that if the Romans found the plan good, it will be so for us."

So we talked of this for a while, and I will say now that in after days we tried it, and the plan worked well enough, at least in the saving of time. Alfred's book learning was ever used for the good of his people, and this was but one way in which he found ready counsel for them.

This was pleasant talk enough, and neither I nor the king grew weary thereof, but the good monk slept at last, and presently the darkness fell, and Alfred dismissed him.

One came and lit the torches on the wall, and still we spoke of my work, until at last Alfred said:

"So you must be busy, and I am glad. When will you set out, and where will you go first?"

Now what I wanted to ask him was where Osmund the jarl had gone. He had ridden to Taunton from Aller, that he might be present at Thora's christening, and that their chrism loosing [lxix] might be held at the same time; and I had looked to find both here, but they were gone. Nor had they left any word for me, and I was troubled about that. So I was about to tell the king what was in my mind concerning Thora first of all, and my heart began to beat strangely. But he waited not for me to answer him.

"Stay," he said, smiling a little. "Before you go I must have a hostage from my wild viking, lest he be, as it were, let loose on the high seas where I cannot reach him."

Then he laughed, at my puzzled face, I suppose, and I saw that he had some jest that pleased him.

"What hostage can I give, lord king?" I said. "Shall I leave Harek and his harp with you?"

"Harek would charm our ears, and would escape," Alfred answered. "Nay, but I must give you house and lands for a home, and therein you shall leave a fair wife, whose loneliness will bring you ashore now and then."

I thought there was more to come, and I liked not this at all, for it went too closely with my fears of what might be. So I bowed, and answered nothing as yet, while he looked laughingly at me.

"Why," he cried, "half my thanes would have gone wild with joy if I had promised them either half of what I have said I would give to you. Are you so fond of the longships and the restless waves that you will not be bound to the shore?"

"Nay, my king," I said; "but I cannot yet rightly understand all that you mean for me."

"Well, it means that I must find you a rich wife, as I think I can. What say you to that fair lady of Exeter town and Taunton--Odda's daughter, Etheldreda?"

"My king," I answered, somewhat over-gladly maybe, "Ethelnoth of Somerset, my good comrade, might have some grudge against me if I cast favouring eyes in that direction. Let this bide for a little while, I pray you, King Alfred. Yet I would not have you think me ungrateful, for indeed I know well what kindness is in your thought for me."

"Nay, but I have it in my mind that you were fond of going to Taunton not so long since, and one might well think that a maiden's hair drew you. Well, if Ethelnoth has outdone you there, I am sorry for your sake, not his. Cheer up, nevertheless. There are more maidens and well dowered in our broad Wessex coasts, and I am minded to see how far you will obey your new overlord."

"This is great kindness, King Alfred," I answered; "but we Northmen are apt to keep some matters wherein to prove our freedom. I pray you not to press this on me."

"Faith," he said, as if to himself, "this viking might be in love already, so wrathful grows he--

"Now, Ranald, it is true that I have set my mind on your wedding a maiden who is rich, and dowered with a coast town, and a good harbour, moreover, where you might keep all your ships under your own eye. I would not have you disappoint me so soon."

Then I said plainly,

"King Alfred, I am loth to do so. But from the very first day that I set foot in England there has been one maiden whose ways have seemed to be bound up with my own, and I can wed none but her. If it does not seem good to you that I should do so now, let me wait till times have grown easier between Saxon and Dane. I think that you may know well that I shall fight none the worse for you if I must strive to win your consent."

"That is straightforward," he said, smiling as if he would seem content. "Let it be so. But it is only fair that before we close this bargain you should see the well-dowered fair lady of whom I speak."

"I will do so if this matter is unknown to her," I answered, "else would be trouble, perhaps, and discomfort. But it is of no use. I have eyes and heart but for that one. Do I know the lady already, perhaps?"

"I believe that you may do so," Alfred said, looking grieved, in a strange way, as if he were half minded to laugh at me for all his seeming vexation. "Odda says that you do, and so also says Etheldreda. Her name is Thora, daughter of Jarl Osmund, and she will have Wareham town and Poole in right of her marriage, as dower to her and to my sea captain."

So spoke the king quickly, and then he could make pretence no longer, but laughed joyously, putting his hands on my shoulders and shaking me a little, while he cried:

"Ay, Ranald; I did but play with you. True lover you are indeed, as I thought. If you are faithful to the king as to the maiden of your choice, both she and I are happy, and it is well."

Then I knew not how to thank him; but he said that Etheldreda and Odda, Heregar and the Lady Alswythe, and maybe Guthrum also, as Thora's guardian, were to be thanked as well.

"You have found many friends here in England already, Ranald my cousin," Alfred said. "Wait until you meet some gathering of them all at Wareham, presently perhaps, where Osmund and Thora are preparing for a wedding--and then make a great thanking if you will, and save words. But I wonder that I have never heard of this matter from you before, for we have been close comrades."

"You must have heard thereof today, my king," I answered; "and you were but beforehand with me. I could speak of such things now that peace has come. Yet I feared that you would be against my wedding a Danish lady."

"It was a natural thought," answered Alfred; "but Thora and Osmund are ours, surely. Perhaps I should have doubted were your mind set on any other. But I have no fears for you."

Then he pondered a little, and went on:

"You say that peace has come. So it has--for a time; and had we to do only with the force that is in England now, I think it would grow and strengthen. We cannot drive out the Danes, and there is room in England for both them and us, and in the days to come the difference of race will be forgotten--not in our time, Ranald, but hereafter, as long years go by. Some day one of my line, if God will, shall reign alone over a united England, stronger for the new blood that has come among us. But it is a great charge that I give to you, Ranald. What we have to fear are the new hosts that come from Denmark, and only a strong fleet can stay them from our shores. I can deal with those who are here, and these in time will help me against fresh comers to the land. There is that in English soil that makes every settler an Englishman in heart. But there is warfare before us yet, and the fleet must break the force of the storm, if it cannot altogether turn it aside."

Then his grave voice changed, and he laughed.

"Heavy things are these to speak in the ears of a bridegroom, but you know all I mean. Now go your ways, and seek Odda, who will rejoice to see you; for word comes from him that his master, Thord the viking, is saying hard things to him because the men do not come in readily to man the ships. At the summer's end I shall be in Winchester, and thence I will come to Wareham to see the fleet, and your wedding also. Go now, and all good go with you."

So Alfred the king set me forth in brotherly wise, speaking on the morrow to my men to bid them serve him and England well under me. And after that all came to pass as the king had planned, and at the summer's end there was a bright wedding for us in Wareham town, while in the wide haven rode at anchor the best fleet that England had ever seen.

So that is how I came to be called "King Alfred's Viking," and made this land my home. What this Wessex fleet of mine has done since those days has been written by others in better words than I can compass; and Harek, whom they call "King Alfred's Scald" nowadays, has made song of what he has seen at my side in English waters; and more he may have to make yet, for the North has not yet sent forth all her hosts. Only I will say this, that if we have not been altogether able to stay the coming of new Danish fleets to the long seaboard that must needs lie open to them here and there till our own fleets are greater, at least they know that the host may no longer come and go as they will, for Alfred's ships have to be reckoned with.

Now of ourselves I will add that Thora and I have many friends, but the best and closest are those whom we made in the days when Hubba came and fell under the shadow of the Quantock Hills, and they do not forget us.

Into our house sometimes come Heregar and Ethered, Denewulf the wise and humble, Odda, and many more, sure of welcome. Only the loved presence of Neot the holy is wanting, for he died in Cornwall in that year of the end of the troubles, and I think that in him I lost more than any save Alfred himself.

Osmund went back to East Anglia for a time, but there he grew wearied with the wrangling of the Danish chiefs as they shared out the new land between them; so he bides with us, finding all his pleasure in the life of farm and field, which is ever near to the heart of a Dane. With him goes old Thord, grumbling at the thralls in strange sea language, and yet well loved. Not until he was wounded sorely in a sea fight we had and won under the Isle of Wight would he leave the war deck; but even now he is the first on board when the ships come home, and he is the one who orders all for winter quarters or for sailing.

Now for long I would that I might look once more on Einar of the Orkneys, my kind foster father, who still bided there in peace, hearing of him now and then as some Norse ship, on her way to join Rolf's fleet in the new land of the Northmen beyond our narrow seas, put into our haven for repair, perhaps after the long voyage, or to see if King Alfred would hire her men for a cruise against the common foe--the Danes. And it was not until the news of his death came thus to me that the home longing for the old lands altogether left me; but since that day my thoughts have been, and will be, for England only. I have no thought or wish that I were sharer in Rolf's victories, nor have my comrades, Harek and Kolgrim and Thord; for we have with Alfred more than the viking could have given us.

I suppose that in days to come out of this long strife shall be wrought new strength and oneness for England, even as Alfred in his wisdom foresees; but as yet sword Helmbiter must be kept sharp, and the ships must be ever ready. But unless the wisdom of Alfred is forgotten, there will never again be wanting a ship captain of English race, as when I, a stranger, was called to the charge of the king's ships in Wessex. The old love of the sea is waking in the hearts of the sons of Hengist.

Therefore I am content, for here have I found the sweetest wife, and the noblest master, and the fairest land that man could wish. And the fear of the old gods is taken from me, and to me has come honour, and somewhat of the joy of victory in a good cause--the cause of freedom and of peace.

Now I write these things as springtime grows apace, and at any time--today, or tomorrow, or next day--into our hall may come Kolgrim my comrade, his scarred face bright with the light of coming battle, to say that Danish ships are once more on the gannet's path; and the sword of Sigurd will rattle in the golden scabbard, and a great English cheer will come from the haven, for King Alfred's ships are ready.

The End.

Notes.

i A Norse homestead consisted of several buildings--the great hall standing alone and apart from the domestic arrangements.

ii The Norse assembly, corresponding to a Saxon "Folkmote," or representative council for a district.

iii Unearthly. The trolls were the demons of the Northern mythology.

iv Byrnie, the close-fitting mail shirt.

v The consecrated silver ring kept in the temple of the district, and worn by the godar, or priest, at all assemblies where it might be necessary to administer an oath. Odin, Frey, and Niord were always called to witness an oath on this ring.

vi God-rede = "good counsel," or "God's counsel," as Alfred means "elves' counsel."

vii Asser's "Life of Alfred." This illness never left the king from his twentieth year to his death. Probably it was neuralgic, as it seems to have been violent pain without lasting effect.

viii This was called "prime signing," and was practically the admission of the heathen as a catechumen.

ix The "Havamal" was the Northern poem which practically embodied the ancient code of morals and behaviour.

x The use of bells was popular early in England, and not less so because a freeman who could afford to build a church with a bell tower became a thane in consequence.

xi The national representative assembly, and origin of our parliament.

xii Now Normandy, and so called after Rolf's Northmen.

xiii This charm against the "evil eye" was used in the west of England until quite lately, and may still linger. The charm against sprains is one yet recorded in the original tongue.

xiv Alfred had Denewulf instructed, and made him Bishop of Winchester.

xv In 845 A.D. Bishop Eahlstan and the levies of Somerset and Dorset defeated the first Danes who landed in Wessex, at the mouth of the Parret.

xvi Trading vessel, more heavily built than the swift longships.

xvii The "wild hunt" is still believed to pass over Cannington and the Quantock Hills, the sounds of the migration of flocks of sea fowl probably keeping the tradition alive.

xviii Athelstan = "noble stone."

xix Confirmation.

End of Project Gutenberg's King Alfred's Viking, by Charles W. Whistler

*** END OF THIS PROJECT GUTENBERG EBOOK KING ALFRED'S VIKING ***

***** This file should be named 14034-h.htm or 14034-h.zip *****
This and all associated files of various formats will be found in:
        http://www.gutenberg.net/1/4/0/3/14034/

Produced by Martin Robb

Updated editions will replace the previous one--the old editions
will be renamed.

Creating the works from public domain print editions means that no
one owns a United States copyright in these works, so the Foundation
(and you!) can copy and distribute it in the United States without
permission and without paying copyright royalties. Special rules,
set forth in the General Terms of Use part of this license, apply to
copying and distributing Project Gutenberg-tm electronic works to
protect the PROJECT GUTENBERG-tm concept and trademark. Project
Gutenberg is a registered trademark, and may not be used if you
charge for the eBooks, unless you receive specific permission. If you
do not charge anything for copies of this eBook, complying with the
rules is very easy. You may use this eBook for nearly any purpose
such as creation of derivative works, reports, performances and
research. They may be modified and printed and given away--you may do
practically ANYTHING with public domain eBooks. Redistribution is
subject to the trademark license, especially commercial
redistribution.

*** START: FULL LICENSE ***

THE FULL PROJECT GUTENBERG LICENSE
PLEASE READ THIS BEFORE YOU DISTRIBUTE OR USE THIS WORK

To protect the Project Gutenberg-tm mission of promoting the free
distribution of electronic works, by using or distributing this work

(or any other work associated in any way with the phrase "Project
Gutenberg"), you agree to comply with all the terms of the Full Project
Gutenberg-tm License (available with this file or online at
http://gutenberg.net/license).

Section 1. General Terms of Use and Redistributing Project Gutenberg-tm
electronic works

1.A. By reading or using any part of this Project Gutenberg-tm
electronic work, you indicate that you have read, understand, agree to
and accept all the terms of this license and intellectual property
(trademark/copyright) agreement. If you do not agree to abide by all
the terms of this agreement, you must cease using and return or destroy
all copies of Project Gutenberg-tm electronic works in your possession.
If you paid a fee for obtaining a copy of or access to a Project
Gutenberg-tm electronic work and you do not agree to be bound by the
terms of this agreement, you may obtain a refund from the person or
entity to whom you paid the fee as set forth in paragraph 1.E.8.

1.B. "Project Gutenberg" is a registered trademark. It may only be
used on or associated in any way with an electronic work by people who
agree to be bound by the terms of this agreement. There are a few
things that you can do with most Project Gutenberg-tm electronic works
even without complying with the full terms of this agreement. See
paragraph 1.C below. There are a lot of things you can do with Project
Gutenberg-tm electronic works if you follow the terms of this agreement
and help preserve free future access to Project Gutenberg-tm electronic
works. See paragraph 1.E below.

1.C. The Project Gutenberg Literary Archive Foundation ("the Foundation"
or PGLAF), owns a compilation copyright in the collection of Project
Gutenberg-tm electronic works. Nearly all the individual works in the
collection are in the public domain in the United States. If an
individual work is in the public domain in the United States and you are
located in the United States, we do not claim a right to prevent you from
copying, distributing, performing, displaying or creating derivative
works based on the work as long as all references to Project Gutenberg
are removed. Of course, we hope that you will support the Project
Gutenberg-tm mission of promoting free access to electronic works by
freely sharing Project Gutenberg-tm works in compliance with the terms of
this agreement for keeping the Project Gutenberg-tm name associated with
the work. You can easily comply with the terms of this agreement by
keeping this work in the same format with its attached full Project
Gutenberg-tm License when you share it without charge with others.

1.D. The copyright laws of the place where you are located also govern
what you can do with this work. Copyright laws in most countries are in
a constant state of change. If you are outside the United States, check
the laws of your country in addition to the terms of this agreement
before downloading, copying, displaying, performing, distributing or
creating derivative works based on this work or any other Project
Gutenberg-tm work. The Foundation makes no representations concerning
the copyright status of any work in any country outside the United
States.

1.E. Unless you have removed all references to Project Gutenberg:

1.E.1. The following sentence, with active links to, or other immediate
access to, the full Project Gutenberg-tm License must appear prominently
whenever any copy of a Project Gutenberg-tm work (any work on which the
phrase "Project Gutenberg" appears, or with which the phrase "Project
Gutenberg" is associated) is accessed, displayed, performed, viewed,
copied or distributed:

This eBook is for the use of anyone anywhere at no cost and with
almost no restrictions whatsoever. You may copy it, give it away or
re-use it under the terms of the Project Gutenberg License included
with this eBook or online at www.gutenberg.net

1.E.2. If an individual Project Gutenberg-tm electronic work is derived
from the public domain (does not contain a notice indicating that it is
posted with permission of the copyright holder), the work can be copied
and distributed to anyone in the United States without paying any fees
or charges. If you are redistributing or providing access to a work
with the phrase "Project Gutenberg" associated with or appearing on the
work, you must comply either with the requirements of paragraphs 1.E.1
through 1.E.7 or obtain permission for the use of the work and the
Project Gutenberg-tm trademark as set forth in paragraphs 1.E.8 or
1.E.9.

1.E.3. If an individual Project Gutenberg-tm electronic work is posted
with the permission of the copyright holder, your use and distribution
must comply with both paragraphs 1.E.1 through 1.E.7 and any additional
terms imposed by the copyright holder. Additional terms will be linked
to the Project Gutenberg-tm License for all works posted with the
permission of the copyright holder found at the beginning of this work.

1.E.4. Do not unlink or detach or remove the full Project Gutenberg-tm
License terms from this work, or any files containing a part of this
work or any other work associated with Project Gutenberg-tm.

1.E.5. Do not copy, display, perform, distribute or redistribute this
electronic work, or any part of this electronic work, without
prominently displaying the sentence set forth in paragraph 1.E.1 with
active links or immediate access to the full terms of the Project
Gutenberg-tm License.

1.E.6. You may convert to and distribute this work in any binary,
compressed, marked up, nonproprietary or proprietary form, including any
word processing or hypertext form. However, if you provide access to or
distribute copies of a Project Gutenberg-tm work in a format other than
"Plain Vanilla ASCII" or other format used in the official version
posted on the official Project Gutenberg-tm web site (www.gutenberg.net),
you must, at no additional cost, fee or expense to the user, provide a
copy, a means of exporting a copy, or a means of obtaining a copy upon
request, of the work in its original "Plain Vanilla ASCII" or other
form. Any alternate format must include the full Project Gutenberg-tm
License as specified in paragraph 1.E.1.

1.E.7. Do not charge a fee for access to, viewing, displaying,
performing, copying or distributing any Project Gutenberg-tm works

unless you comply with paragraph 1.E.8 or 1.E.9.

1.E.8. You may charge a reasonable fee for copies of or providing access to or distributing Project Gutenberg-tm electronic works provided that

- You pay a royalty fee of 20% of the gross profits you derive from the use of Project Gutenberg-tm works calculated using the method you already use to calculate your applicable taxes. The fee is owed to the owner of the Project Gutenberg-tm trademark, but he has agreed to donate royalties under this paragraph to the Project Gutenberg Literary Archive Foundation. Royalty payments must be paid within 60 days following each date on which you prepare (or are legally required to prepare) your periodic tax returns. Royalty payments should be clearly marked as such and sent to the Project Gutenberg Literary Archive Foundation at the address specified in Section 4, "Information about donations to the Project Gutenberg Literary Archive Foundation."

- You provide a full refund of any money paid by a user who notifies you in writing (or by e-mail) within 30 days of receipt that s/he does not agree to the terms of the full Project Gutenberg-tm License. You must require such a user to return or
destroy all copies of the works possessed in a physical medium and discontinue all use of and all access to other copies of Project Gutenberg-tm works.

- You provide, in accordance with paragraph 1.F.3, a full refund of any money paid for a work or a replacement copy, if a defect in the electronic work is discovered and reported to you within 90 days of receipt of the work.

- You comply with all other terms of this agreement for free distribution of Project Gutenberg-tm works.

1.E.9. If you wish to charge a fee or distribute a Project Gutenberg-tm electronic work or group of works on different terms than are set forth in this agreement, you must obtain permission in writing from both the Project Gutenberg Literary Archive Foundation and Michael Hart, the owner of the Project Gutenberg-tm trademark. Contact the Foundation as set forth in Section 3 below.

1.F.

1.F.1. Project Gutenberg volunteers and employees expend considerable effort to identify, do copyright research on, transcribe and proofread public domain works in creating the Project Gutenberg-tm
collection. Despite these efforts, Project Gutenberg-tm electronic works, and the medium on which they may be stored, may contain "Defects," such as, but not limited to, incomplete, inaccurate or corrupt data, transcription errors, a copyright or other intellectual property infringement, a defective or damaged disk or other medium, a computer virus, or computer codes that damage or cannot be read by your equipment.

1.F.2. LIMITED WARRANTY, DISCLAIMER OF DAMAGES - Except for the "Right

of Replacement or Refund" described in paragraph 1.F.3, the Project
Gutenberg Literary Archive Foundation, the owner of the Project
Gutenberg-tm trademark, and any other party distributing a Project
Gutenberg-tm electronic work under this agreement, disclaim all
liability to you for damages, costs and expenses, including legal
fees. YOU AGREE THAT YOU HAVE NO REMEDIES FOR NEGLIGENCE, STRICT
LIABILITY, BREACH OF WARRANTY OR BREACH OF CONTRACT EXCEPT THOSE
PROVIDED IN PARAGRAPH F3. YOU AGREE THAT THE FOUNDATION, THE
TRADEMARK OWNER, AND ANY DISTRIBUTOR UNDER THIS AGREEMENT WILL NOT BE
LIABLE TO YOU FOR ACTUAL, DIRECT, INDIRECT, CONSEQUENTIAL, PUNITIVE OR
INCIDENTAL DAMAGES EVEN IF YOU GIVE NOTICE OF THE POSSIBILITY OF SUCH
DAMAGE.

1.F.3. LIMITED RIGHT OF REPLACEMENT OR REFUND - If you discover a
defect in this electronic work within 90 days of receiving it, you can
receive a refund of the money (if any) you paid for it by sending a
written explanation to the person you received the work from. If you
received the work on a physical medium, you must return the medium with
your written explanation. The person or entity that provided you with
the defective work may elect to provide a replacement copy in lieu of a
refund. If you received the work electronically, the person or entity
providing it to you may choose to give you a second opportunity to
receive the work electronically in lieu of a refund. If the second copy
is also defective, you may demand a refund in writing without further
opportunities to fix the problem.

1.F.4. Except for the limited right of replacement or refund set forth
in paragraph 1.F.3, this work is provided to you 'AS-IS' WITH NO OTHER
WARRANTIES OF ANY KIND, EXPRESS OR IMPLIED, INCLUDING BUT NOT LIMITED TO
WARRANTIES OF MERCHANTIBILITY OR FITNESS FOR ANY PURPOSE.

1.F.5. Some states do not allow disclaimers of certain implied
warranties or the exclusion or limitation of certain types of damages.
If any disclaimer or limitation set forth in this agreement violates the
law of the state applicable to this agreement, the agreement shall be
interpreted to make the maximum disclaimer or limitation permitted by
the applicable state law. The invalidity or unenforceability of any
provision of this agreement shall not void the remaining provisions.

1.F.6. INDEMNITY - You agree to indemnify and hold the Foundation, the
trademark owner, any agent or employee of the Foundation, anyone
providing copies of Project Gutenberg-tm electronic works in accordance
with this agreement, and any volunteers associated with the production,
promotion and distribution of Project Gutenberg-tm electronic works,
harmless from all liability, costs and expenses, including legal fees,
that arise directly or indirectly from any of the following which you do
or cause to occur: (a) distribution of this or any Project Gutenberg-tm
work, (b) alteration, modification, or additions or deletions to any
Project Gutenberg-tm work, and (c) any Defect you cause.

Section 2. Information about the Mission of Project Gutenberg-tm

Project Gutenberg-tm is synonymous with the free distribution of
electronic works in formats readable by the widest variety of computers
including obsolete, old, middle-aged and new computers. It exists

because of the efforts of hundreds of volunteers and donations from
people in all walks of life.

Volunteers and financial support to provide volunteers with the
assistance they need, is critical to reaching Project Gutenberg-tm's
goals and ensuring that the Project Gutenberg-tm collection will
remain freely available for generations to come. In 2001, the Project
Gutenberg Literary Archive Foundation was created to provide a secure
and permanent future for Project Gutenberg-tm and future generations.
To learn more about the Project Gutenberg Literary Archive Foundation
and how your efforts and donations can help, see Sections 3 and 4
and the Foundation web page at http://www.pglaf.org.

Section 3. Information about the Project Gutenberg Literary Archive
Foundation

The Project Gutenberg Literary Archive Foundation is a non profit
501(c)(3) educational corporation organized under the laws of the
state of Mississippi and granted tax exempt status by the Internal
Revenue Service. The Foundation's EIN or federal tax identification
number is 64-6221541. Its 501(c)(3) letter is posted at
http://pglaf.org/fundraising. Contributions to the Project Gutenberg
Literary Archive Foundation are tax deductible to the full extent
permitted by U.S. federal laws and your state's laws.

The Foundation's principal office is located at 4557 Melan Dr. S.
Fairbanks, AK, 99712., but its volunteers and employees are scattered
throughout numerous locations. Its business office is located at
809 North 1500 West, Salt Lake City, UT 84116, (801) 596-1887, email
business@pglaf.org. Email contact links and up to date contact
information can be found at the Foundation's web site and official
page at http://pglaf.org

For additional contact information:
    Dr. Gregory B. Newby
    Chief Executive and Director
    gbnewby@pglaf.org

Section 4. Information about Donations to the Project Gutenberg
Literary Archive Foundation

Project Gutenberg-tm depends upon and cannot survive without wide
spread public support and donations to carry out its mission of
increasing the number of public domain and licensed works that can be
freely distributed in machine readable form accessible by the widest
array of equipment including outdated equipment. Many small donations
($1 to $5,000) are particularly important to maintaining tax exempt
status with the IRS.

The Foundation is committed to complying with the laws regulating
charities and charitable donations in all 50 states of the United
States. Compliance requirements are not uniform and it takes a
considerable effort, much paperwork and many fees to meet and keep up
with these requirements. We do not solicit donations in locations

where we have not received written confirmation of compliance. To
SEND DONATIONS or determine the status of compliance for any
particular state visit http://pglaf.org

While we cannot and do not solicit contributions from states where we
have not met the solicitation requirements, we know of no prohibition
against accepting unsolicited donations from donors in such states who
approach us with offers to donate.

International donations are gratefully accepted, but we cannot make
any statements concerning tax treatment of donations received from
outside the United States. U.S. laws alone swamp our small staff.

Please check the Project Gutenberg Web pages for current donation
methods and addresses. Donations are accepted in a number of other
ways including including checks, online payments and credit card
donations. To donate, please visit: http://pglaf.org/donate

Section 5. General Information About Project Gutenberg-tm electronic
works.

Professor Michael S. Hart is the originator of the Project Gutenberg-tm
concept of a library of electronic works that could be freely shared
with anyone. For thirty years, he produced and distributed Project
Gutenberg-tm eBooks with only a loose network of volunteer support.

Project Gutenberg-tm eBooks are often created from several printed
editions, all of which are confirmed as Public Domain in the U.S.
unless a copyright notice is included. Thus, we do not necessarily
keep eBooks in compliance with any particular paper edition.

Most people start at our Web site which has the main PG search facility:

     http://www.gutenberg.net

This Web site includes information about Project Gutenberg-tm,
including how to make donations to the Project Gutenberg Literary
Archive Foundation, how to help produce our new eBooks, and how to
subscribe to our email newsletter to hear about new eBooks.